REPRESENTATION AND
ADMINISTRATIVE TRIBUNALS

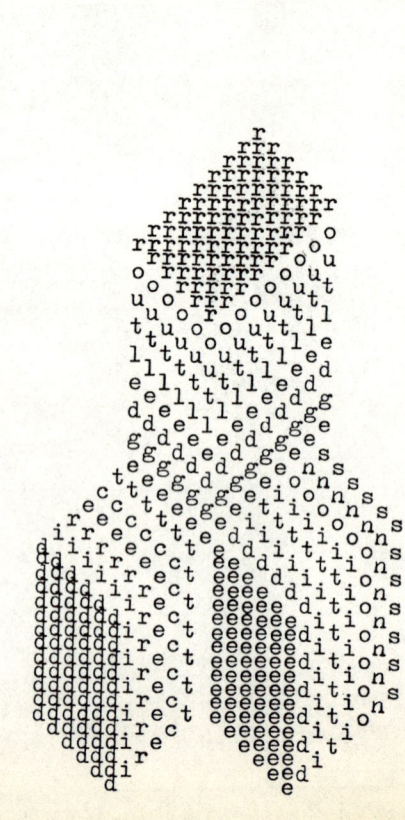

REPRESENTATION AND ADMINISTRATIVE TRIBUNALS

ANNE FROST

and

CORAL HOWARD

ROUTLEDGE DIRECT EDITIONS

ROUTLEDGE & KEGAN PAUL
London, Henley and Boston

First published in 1977
by Routledge & Kegan Paul Ltd
39 Store Street,
London WC1E 7DD,
Broadway House,
Newtown Road,
Henley-on-Thames,
Oxon RG9 1EN and
9 Park Street,
Boston, Mass. 02108, USA
Printed and bound in Great Britain by
Lowe & Brydone Printers Ltd,
Thetford, Norfolk

British Library Cataloguing in Publication Data

Frost, Anne
    Representation and administrative tribunals.
    1. Administrative courts - England
    I. Title II. Howard, Coral
    342'.42'066   KD4890   77-30219

    ISBN 0-7100-8701-2

CONTENTS

TABLES

FOREWORD

This volume reports on one of a series of research projects carried out by the Legal Advice Research Unit (LARU) during the period 1971-4. (1) The Unit was set up and financed by the Nuffield Foundation in response to a growing concern on the part of certain practising lawyers, legal academics, social workers and many others, regarding the provision of legal services. Imbued with the spirit of Beveridge, (2) post-war England had emerged as a state where the involvement of government in the day-to-day lives of the vast majority of citizens became a highly significant factor. The rise of the 'welfare state', which Marshall saw as a process of conferring the rights of citizenry on the working class, (3) entailed the widespread provision of services which not only affected the standard of living of individuals, but equally importantly, substantially increased peoples' expectations. (4)

However, disillusionment with the welfare philosophy on which post-war legislation had been based grew during the late 1950s and 1960s at which period poverty was 'rediscovered' in supposedly affluent Britain, (5) and other features of the welfare state such as education and housing, were shown to be seriously flawed by continued inequality and inadequacy. (6) Despite such recognition, there was little fundamental or radical questioning of the nature of the services provided, nor of the manner in which they were obtainable. The debate tended to centre around arguments such as 'universalism' versus 'selectivism' in the allocation of scarce resources, and criticism was directed more at the implementation of welfare policies rather than at their philosophy.

During this same period, similar dissatisfaction with prevailing conditions was being experienced in the USA where, in response to inner-city problems, the Civil Rights Movement grew rapidly, and, combined with the pressures exerted by grassroot organisations, led to the government of that country instigating the 'War on Poverty'. But the area of questioning in the two countries differed somewhat and, initially at least, resulted in different types of solutions. Whereas in Britain the amount and extent of provisions led to an examination of the economic relations between the state and the individual, in the USA the concern was more with the form and administration of provisions, and led to an attempt at a more directly political

solution regarding the rights and obligations conferred on individuals by the state.

In the USA the passing of the Equal Opportunity Act in 1964
led to the establishment of programmes such as OEO which adopted
an increasingly militant stance and consistently challenged both
federal and state governments. (7) These developments were
accompanied by a recognition of the relationship between law and
social change, and furthermore were not confined to academic debate,
but also took place at the level of 'law in action'. One of the
results was the setting up of a wide network of legal services, a
situation reflected in amendments to the Act in 1965.

Such developments were slow to reach Britain where, as was
earlier argued, more attention had consistently been paid to the
economic rather than to the political aspects of inequality and
deprivation. Nevertheless in both countries legal services were
added to the spectrum of welfare services under criticism.

At the same time a small proportion of British social Workers
were questioning the philosophy underlying much current social work
practice. (8) There was concern about the way in which success as
a social worker was often achieved by persuading clients to redefine
the problem or to 'accommodate' to the situation, (9) and there
emerged a growing awareness that the structure of society might have
an important bearing on the ills faced by individual clients. As the
concept of welfare rights began to replace earlier views of welfare
as a privilege, so the legal implications of social work practice
came increasingly to the fore. Although it took rather longer for
lawyers to address themselves to similar questions, some of the
younger members, led by a relatively small but influential number
of politically involved lawyers and legal academics, moved slowly
in the same direction and began to address themselves to the relationship between law and social change.

It was against this background that LARU was set up, under the
general guidance of an Advisory Committee representing a wide range
of interests. This committee proposed that the Unit should address
itself to the problem of unmet needs and should concern itself with
two main questions:

(a)   What is the nature and extent of the various needs for legal
      advice and assistance?
(b)   How are these needs best met?

Their proposal arose out of the perceived importance of improving
access to legal services, combined with a belief that inequality
of access was largely a function of differential income, as well
as the inappropriate location of lawyers' offices and the middle-
class image projected by the profession. (10) It was hoped initially
that the Research Unit would be in a position to evaluate a number
of experimental schemes designed to improve the access to legal
services, and would then be able to provide policy makers with
guidance, thereby paving the way for government intervention.

At the outset, and throughout the existence of the Unit, the
validity of accepting the lawyers' definition of legal need was
questioned by the researchers. Three issues seemed crucial:
first, the recognition that legal needs cannot be defined in any

absolute sense; second, that they are socially defined; and third,
that they cannot be isolated from the broader concept of social
need. Since that time, such views have become much more generally
accepted, (11) but when LARU first came into existence there was a
tendency for most lawyers to regard questions of this nature with
considerable suspicion. However, there are strong indications that
the full implications of broadening the area of debate in this way
are still not fully recognised, and in particular, there is often
an important misconception with regard to the overlapping nature of
legal and social need.

For the lawyer, the definition of legal need relates to those
frustrations which people suffer, and which are amenable to
amelioration by the law as laid down in statute. Social need -
as viewed by the legal profession - generally relates to those
frustrations that cannot be so ameliorated, and which have to be
dealt with otherwise than by the enforcement of the law. Whilst
an increasing number of lawyers recognise that the two are often
interacting and overlapping, they nevertheless believe that 'professionals' or 'experts' can diagnose the presenting problem in
such a way as to ensure that it is dealt with by the appropriate
profession, and in the 'right' way. Such a definition effectively
closes the options available to the client by enabling the profession to control both its input and its output: in so doing, the
mystification of the profession is perpetuated. Furthermore by
limiting the areas of need which are encompassed within the framework of legal services (12) the danger of lawyers being required
to adopt a more political stance (as has happened in the USA) is
greatly reduced. (13) Perhaps most importantly, in so far as the
service offered in response even to those problems defined by the
profession as legal is a reactive rather than a proactive one, the
role of law as an agent of social change is considerably curtailed.

Arising from this broader view of the research task than that
originally envisaged by the Advisory Committee, the staff of LARU
always worked towards trying to achieve both a greater appreciation
of the social definition of legal needs, and a better understanding
of the structural reasons for inequality of access to the law.

Whilst concentrating on the question of representation in a
quasi-legal setting, the study of administrative tribunals reported
here reviews the differing perspectives of all the participants in
the tribunal process: chairmen and members, appellants and representatives. The approach used is essentially sociological;
through an examination of the backgrounds and general life situation of each group, an attempt is made to assess how these impinge
on their particular approach to the tribunal process. Although
the method of study adopted depends more on survey techniques than
had originally been intended (owing largely to outside pressures
exerted on the team) (14) the aim remains one of looking beyond
particular tribunal hearings when considering the perceptions of the
different actors. The fact that they all converged at a particular
point in time to deal with one particular problem is important, but
even more crucial for the research team was the wish to look at how,
and why, each of them arrived there. It is a comparative approach
rather than one which attempts to explain, though perhaps it would
be more accurate to describe the research as an account of the

processes at work in certain administrative tribunals.

In selecting for study three different types of welfare tribunals; Supplementary Benefit Appeals Tribunals, National Insurance
Local Tribunals and Rent Tribunals, the authors took as their starting point the 'advantages' of administrative tribunals over courts
(as identified in the Franks Report); namely speed, informality,
cheapness and freedom from technicality. (15) Their findings inevitably lead them to question whether many of the differences between the court system and the tribunal system exist in practice
and, where they do so, whether the tribunal system can legitimately
be regarded as 'advantageous'.

It became evident that two questions needed to be considered
before the role and value of representation could properly be
addressed: first, the extent to which tribunals are truly independent of ministerial control, and second, the degree to which
their decision-making is discretionary. As the authors point out,
the independence of tribunals (16) is a central issue, one affecting
both the degree of impartiality that is maintained and the point at
which discretionary decision-making may become suspect. A wide
range of participants in the tribunal process were found to
seriously doubt the possibility of arriving at 'fair' decisions,
because of the structural weaknesses which exist in maintaining independence from departmental influence at hearings.

With regard to discretion, it is equally questionable whether
it would be advantageous to introduce more legal rules to circum-
scribe the amount of discretion exercised by tribunals, or whether
individualised justice is better served by the present system
which, particularly in some tribunals, maximises the amount of discretion. Nevertheless, whilst recognising that their work is based
on small samples, the authors make a plea for greater control,
either by 'legalising' tribunals (i.e. transforming policies into
rules than bind decision-makers), or by 'judicialising' them (i.e.
making the administrative process similar to the judicial process
in so far as the rules of natural justice are ensured by procedural
devices).

As is discussed in the present study, the Lord Chancellor's
Advisory Committee in its 1973/4 Report suggested that legal aid
should be available for representation at tribunals by qualified
lawyers. At the time of writing, this recommendation has not been
implemented, and the Lord Chancellor has recently said that money
was not at present available for the extension of legal aid to
administrative tribunals, (17) although legal advice for the preparation of case papers for a tribunal hearing is now available
under the £25 scheme. (18)

The authors of this report are in little doubt that representation is indeed a necessary, if short-term, remedy or safeguard
for the individual, particularly when the other party to the dispute
is a government department. However, it is important to note that
they make clear that such representation should not be confined to
legal representation. Given adequate support services by the legal
profession, many other groups such as trade union officials, social
workers and welfare rights groups, as well as articulate and well-
informed individuals, can and do make an important contribution to
the protection of individual interests.

Yet representation alone, even if vastly expanded in scale, will
provide no panacea in the effort to achieve social justice. Given
the existing tribunal system other factors such as panel membership, training, administration and procedure must all be re-
considered if the appellant is to be lifted from an inherently dis-
advantageous position.

To the extent that this study spells out the need for representation and demonstrates its advantages, albeit as a short-term remedy,
we believe the work has contributed to the examination of the 'unmet
need for legal services' as intended by the Advisory Committee.
At the same time the way in which the research was carried out enabled the authors to draw attention to some of the other, more
fundamental issues which, in the context of welfare tribunals, are
relevant to the relationship between law and social change. Their
concern was necessarily with tribunals as they now exist, but their
findings must surely bring into question whether the present
adversarial (19) system (albeit in a somewhat modified form) is the
most suitable arena for conflict-resolution when dealing with welfare matters. Welfare provision does not contain within it the
machinery for changing the basis underlying the present social and
economic system, it simply provides the machinery to make things
run more smoothly, and tribunals act as a safety-net which tries to
ensure that people do not sink to distressingly low levels. Extending representation will do nothing to change this situation, indeed
it will perpetuate the present trend towards the individualisation
of problems and the denial of their socio-economic origins in many
instances.

Given that we live in a highly stratified society the presence
of lawyers and other types of representative at tribunals is a
minimum requirement of social justice. Hopefully, in the process
of representing their clients, those lawyers involved will address
themselves to the need for legislative change at the level of
social policy, including a review of the type of case considered
by welfare tribunals and clarification of legislative intent with
respect to those remaining within their domain. Lawyers should not
be used merely as an appendage to the social services, nor is it
sufficient for them to concern themselves with procedural rights.
Changes in administrative law, particularly as it affects deprived
and vulnerable groups of people, is long overdue and provides an
arena which is new to most lawyers, but nevertheless one of great
importance.

Vancouver, BC, August 1976   Pauline Morris

ACKNOWLEDGMENTS

This study was carried out under the auspices of the Nuffield
Foundation and our first thanks go to that body for making our work
possible.

We also gratefully acknowledge the advice and assistance given
to us at all stages of the study by a variety of other individuals
and organisations.

We offer particular thanks to Susan Newall who acted as a research assistant during the fieldwork, and who was responsible for
all the interviewing and observations of tribunals in the north-
west region. Her interest and enthusiasm provided us with constant
stimulation and support.

We are grateful to the Council of Tribunals for helpful discussions and data provided whilst the project was being designed.
Our thanks also go to the Presidents of the Rent Assessment Panels
who arranged access to the Rent Tribunals in their regions, and for
their advice and comments.

We would like to express particular thanks to the Department of
Health and Social Security, whose officials have been involved at
all stages of the project, from its design to its completion, and
who made many helpful comments on an earlier draft. We would like
to state however that their views on the present conduct of the
tribunals under review differ from ours in important respects.
Consequently any mistakes which appear in the text, and wider
matters of subjective interpretation, remain identified with the
authors.

To the many appellants whose homes we visited, to the tribunal
chairmen and members interviewed and also to the representatives,
we express our thanks.

We are grateful to Mrs Isabel Leung, for typing all our material.
Finally, we acknowledge the guidance, support, criticism and encouragement given to us by Dr Pauline Morris, who in her capacity
as a Research Director had the unenviable task of supervising our
work; and we are particularly grateful for her extensive editing
of an earlier draft, and for providing a foreword to the main text.

London, November 1976   Anne Frost
                                                   Coral Howard

Part one

BACKGROUND TO THE STUDY

Chapter 1

PLANNING THE RESEARCH

The end product of a research project, generally a report such as this, very often presents a static view of what has been essentially a fluid process. This study of administrative tribunals can best be understood in the context of its background. Ideas and events played their part in shaping the research and it is important to draw out for comment some of those influences.

In 1971 the Legal Advice Research Unit embarked on its first projects, studies of unmet need in the field of socio-legal services in two London boroughs. Three points need to be made here about that work. First, it was essentially exploratory in nature, attempting to assess the nature and extent of both needs and existing services (using broad definitions of both). Second, an integral part of the work was the idea of innovation, that is the possible provision by the Nuffield Foundation of some sort of service to help fill the gap between problems and existing services. Third, these first projects each had a firm geographical basis, that is they were located in London and within local governmental administrative boundaries.

The importance of administrative tribunals was recognised in those early projects. Three particular problems had been mentioned as being important: first, the absence in many tribunals of a right of appeal on matters of fact; second, the difficulty of obtaining representation in a situation where legal aid is not available; third, the lack of consistency in decision-making at some types of tribunal. (1)

In the two London boroughs research workers spent short periods of observation at two types of tribunal; Supplementary Benefit Appeal Tribunals and Rent Tribunals. The choice of those tribunals for study did not at the time reflect theoretical considerations per se, but rather considerations of ease of access, time, and relevance to the emphasis of the first year's work.

In spite of the somewhat cursory examination of these tribunals (involving perhaps four weeks' fieldwork), one of the research team became particularly interested in questions posed by the intervention of representation at tribunal hearings. Time did not allow these questions to be pursued in any detail. Concurrently the research team had also become particularly interested in another aspect of the work in the London boroughs, namely the general area of social work

and law. The research team believed that small-scale, intensive
research studies centred on these two theoretical areas could explore
the problems more fully.

Accordingly, a paper was written by the team which drew together
the ideas and problems mentioned above. These small projects were
envisaged as being dependent on ideas rather than places per se,
thereby being freed from the geographical limits of the first year's
studies. In essence, the ideas were accepted as a basis for the
Unit's subsequent work, and amongst others a two-year project was set
up which was to investigate representation at administrative
tribunals.

THE TRIBUNALS UNDER STUDY

In view of the fact that this study was intended to form part of a
wider project concerned with an examination of unmet need, a decision
was made to concentrate upon those tribunals classified as 'welfare'
tribunals, although their ramifications are also economic in essence. (2)
The three selected; National Insurance Local Tribunals, Supplementary
Benefits Appeal Tribunals and Rent Tribunals are ones with which
the average citizen is most likely to become involved should
any dispute arise as to his command, or lack of command, over
welfare resources.   More importantly all three tribunals tend to
relate to crisis points in the appellant's life, when his need or
dependency may be at its greatest due to personal, health, or
economic circumstances.

National Insurance Local Tribunals, of which there were 189 at the
end of 1973, hear appeals from claimants dissatisfied with decisions
of insurance officers and also decide cases referred to them by
insurance officers. During 1973, they dealt with 29,477 appeals, (3)
but this is a mere fraction of the 22 million claims handled by
local officers each year, a figure which indicates the vast involvement of the general population with the range of National Insurance
benefits. Claims cover the following wide-ranging categories:
unemployment benefit, sickness benefit, maternity benefit, widow's
benefit, guardian's allowance, retirement pension, death grant,
child's special allowance, industrial injuries, family allowance,
attendance allowance and invalidity pension.

There are 120 Supplementary Benefit Appeal Tribunals in Britain
and, in 1973, 26,002 cases were cleared. (4) Appeals against
decisions of the local officer of the Supplementary Benefit
Commission mainly concern supplementary pensions and allowances,
exceptional needs payments and benefits in respect of National
Health Services charges. (5) Because of the non-contributory nature
of these benefits, which are intended to provide a temporary 'safety
net' for persons without means of support, a much more restricted
sector of the population at large is eligible for benefits than
would be the case for contribution-based National Insurance provisions. Nevertheless, in November 1973, over $2\frac{1}{2}$ million pople were
receiving supplementary benefits. The groups most likely to be involved tend to comprise the most vulnerable members of our society:
the old, the sick and disabled, women with dependent children and a
relatively small number of the unemployed. Over time, these groups

have demonstrated that their dependency is more than likely to remain
long term, if not permanent.

Since the Second World War, the need for government intervention
in the private contract between landlord and tenant has been
recognised in order to prevent exploitation in a situation of
housing shortage. In 1945, the Ridley Committee recommended the
establishment of local rent tribunals to adjudicate on the levels
of rents to be charged by landords. (6) Control was extended to
furnished houses, and tribunals were to determine what rents were
'reasonable'.

The Rent Tribunal is somewhat different from the other two
tribunals which fall within our study, because it concerns the
resolution of disputes between private individuals, and no government department is party to the conflict. However, in inner-city
areas the issue often devolves on security rather than rent levels
and as such concerns maintenance of access to a social resource and
can be seen as falling within primary welfare provision in the same
way that the other two tribunals concern primary income maintenance.

In 1971, 21,171 cases were heard by Rent Tribunals in respect of
the fixing of rent and security of tenure for occupants of furnished
premises, (7) only 14 per cent of accommodation is privately rented
today; 3.4 per cent is accounted for by furnished lettings which,
until August 1974, came within the separate jurisdiction of the
Rent Tribunal. Rent Tribunals concern relatively small numbers of
applicants, but occupants of furnished premises comprise a specific
group which is particularly vulnerable. Not only has their basic
housing tenure remained insecure until the new legislation was enacted in 1974, but this group tends to suffer on many other indices.
A recent Shelter Report (8) analysed certain background factors relating to applicants to London Rent Tribunals and found that 26 per
cent of the sample comprised single-parent households, two-thirds
of tenants were in furnished accommodation at their previous address
and were being forced to move unwillingly between furnished flats,
and 90 per cent of applications concerned security of tenure. Our
own survey of applicants indicates that 41 per cent of tenants were
dependent on supplementary benefits or national insurance payments
and 46 per cent of respondents stated that they were suffering from
financial hardship.

Previous studies of SBATs have demonstrated that represented
appellants are more successful (in terms of the proportion of
revised decisions) than non-represented appellants. (9) However,
such studies have not extended their investigation beyond the
immediate outcome for appellants in terms of success rates, and
there has been no examination of the long-term consequences on
policy and tribunal decision-making brought about by changing trends
in representation. Some years ago, the Council on Tribunals made
a similar point: 'some research might be concentrating on too
narrow a front and ... it might be better to look more broadly at
the general functioning of a particular class of tribunal and examine the question of assistance in that context, more attention
being paid to lay assistance than is now the case.' (10)

This present study attempts to place an investigation of representation at administrative tribunals within a wider theoretical
context. In selecting the three particular types of tribunals

mentioned above, it examines their relative independence from their respective government departments, the different personnel constituting tribunal membership and the varying degree of discretion available to them. Early observations suggested that these variables were crucial if a discussion of representation was to be extended beyond the immediate outcome for appellants (in terms of success rates) to a consideration of its implications for the tribunals themselves.

The original research proposal suggested a double-edged approach to the problem, and whilst subsequent pressures have in many ways altered the emphasis of the research, this underlying philosophy remained. In the first place, the study examines the relationship between tribunal personnel and the government department to which the tribunal is linked. This part of the study draws much of its data from existing literature and documentation, and presents findings from our own fieldwork within that context.

Second, the study attempts to examine, in some depth, the dynamics of the social processes at work when representation intervenes in the tribunal situation. The interaction between the various parties - tribunal, representative, appellant, government official - are seen as crucial to an understanding of the effects of representation. This part of the study draws its data from the extended interviews which were conducted with the parties concerned, and from observations of tribunal hearings. A more detailed description of the methodology is presented in chapter 2 but it is important to emphasise here that interviews reflected the philosophy underlying the research; namely that representation must be viewed in the total context of the tribunal situation, and that it must be viewed from several different perspectives reflecting the interests of all the parties concerned. Similarly, our observations attempted to assess the roles played by all those present at each tribunal hearing, and how the eventual outcome for the appellant was, at least in part, based on that interaction.

In the early stages of formulating a research design it was felt that the most productive and appropriate approach would be to spend extended periods with relatively few specific tribunals, in order that the research workers might become fully acquainted with the processes at work at individual tribunals. But policy considerations, discussed below, intervened and altered to some extent the method adopted. To those concerned with policy, the sacrifice of 'quantity' in preference to 'depth' is often anathema, since it is widely held that generalisations cannot be based on very small samples. This tends to ignore the fact that generalisations derived from small intensive studies are of a different nature than those based on statistics, being more concerned with understanding the processes at work. In the present study, the research workers' concern to adopt a predominantly qualitative approach to the problem had to give way to policy considerations and this resulted in a more broadly based quantitative study. These shaping influences are now discussed.

INFLUENCES SHAPING THE RESEARCH

An important source of pressure became obvious before the research
design was even completed. In October 1972, the Research Director
and a research officer were invited to give oral evidence to the
Lord Chancellor's Legal Aid Advisory Committee. This evidence was
concerned with a report of our findings in the two London
boroughs relating to the development of legal advice centres.
During the course of giving evidence, the pilot work carried out at
tribunals was mentioned and some impressions given about representation in that situation. There was an immediate and interested response from the Committee; they wanted to know how soon they could
expect results from the proposed tribunals project. The fact that
the project was intended to last two years and that a final report
could not be completed until then seemed to surprise them. They
asked if they could have an interim report on the subject in six
months' time.
      The Lord Chancellor's Advisory Committee's interest in tribunals
is, naturally, specifically oriented towards policy considerations.
In 1968, the Committee had been asked 'whether, if additional funds
were available for legal aid, they were most required to raise the
legal aid limits or to extend legal aid to tribunals and, if legal
aid were extended in this way, before which tribunals it was most
needed'. (11)
      The Committee's original recommendation had been that legal aid
should be extended only to the Lands Tribunals, but by 1972 the
Committee felt that the situation required more detailed consideration. A number of interested organisations (including LARU) were
invited to submit evidence and the Committee proposed to publish a
report later in 1974. (12) The importance of research on this topic
had been stressed (which explains the enthusiastic response to the
news of LARU's proposed research project), but it was clear from
the beginning that our research would not be completed in time. Before fieldwork was even completed, let alone the analysis of data
begun, the Committee urged the LARU team to provide information, the
nature of which had clear policy implications.
      The source of pressure from this direction was, therefore, two-
fold. There was the factor of time, whereby the team had to collect
together ideas, impressions and some evidence before it would normally have done so. There was also the more important factor of
policy. The explicit policy orientation of the Lord Chancellor's
Committee, combined with the implicit policy concerns of LARU's own
consultative committee (a body drawn together to represent a wide
spectrum of interest groups) presented considerable pressure. The
Research Director decided that this project could not depend on a
qualitative approach alone, its scale had to be widened. The expansion of the project was in terms of geography and numbers, but
not in terms of the time available for the research. With limited
time and resources, therefore, some'depth' had of necessity to be
sacrificed for sheer quantity of results.
      The final form of our research was also affected by one of the
main bodies with whom we needed to negotiate, the head office of the
Department of Health and Social Security. This is not to say that
unwelcome pressure was exerted by that body on the LARU team, rather

that in the course of making operational decisions (where the co-
operation of officials was both necessary and advantageous) advice
and practical suggestions were offered which it would have been
foolish to ignore. Details of the decisions which were affected by
our conversations with departmental officials are discussed in the
following chapter, but in terms of the general shape of the project
two factors are important. In the first place, the department was
anxious to facilitate our research and to provide it with official
backing (the Lord Chancellor's Committee's interest and the
Nuffield Foundation's status were probably important motivating
factors) but at the same time it had to protect itself carefully,
particularly with respect to the confidentiality of potential interviewees. Considerable time and energy were therefore expended in
working out precisely how far departmental officials could go in
helping us without jeopardising either their own responsibility for
confidentiality, or our own independent status as research workers.
The second major factor related to officials' concern that we should
'tread softly'. At the time when the research started, local staff
at DHSS offices were operating a policy of 'non-co-operation'
brought about by an industrial dispute, and head office staff were
wary about requiring them to do even a minimum amount of extra work
without first ensuring that this would not provoke a crisis.
Negotiations between head office and their regional offices were
therefore somewhat protracted, and had the effect of cutting down
the time available for fieldwork. Officials were also anxious that
we should 'tread softly' with regard to certain tribunal chairmen
and members, who were going through a phase of acute sensitivity
at the time following the attention of other research workers. This
affected to some extent the choice of tribunals to be studied and
also the type of questions to be asked.
    The resulting design of the project shows the effect of the in-
fluences described above. Many of its features now more closely
resemble a survey than had been intended originally, but throughout
the project we have been concerned to preserve, as far as possible,
the original perspectives from which our interest in this area
grew. In the following chapter we outline the form which the study
took and present in more detail the perspectives underlying the
research.

CHAPTER 2

THE STUDY

CHOICE OF TRIBUNALS

The choice of tribunals to be included in a study of representation
involves two broad problems. In the first place, there is no single
'type' of representation which is found at all tribunals. Second,
there is no simple 'effect' of representation which is true for all
tribunals. Whilst the first problem involves a consideration of
different forms of representation and different types of representative, the second draws into question the characteristics of the
tribunals themselves. The implications of these problems in design-
ing the present study are set out below.

Apart from the traditional (although rare) representation conducted by lawyers at tribunals, there has been evidence during recent
years of an increasing interest in such work amongst non-legal
groups. These groups include a few from statutory services (social
workers, probation officers) and many more from non-statutory
sources (Claimants Unions, Citizens Rights Offices, Housing Aid
Centres). Observations at SBATs and Rent Tribunals during the
earlier studies of the London boroughs, suggested that tribunals did
not react uniformly to different types of representatives and
different styles of representation. Furthermore, it was apparent
that in some circumstances, the tribunal's reaction to a representative depended not so much on the characteristics of that representative as on certain characteristics of the tribunal.

For example, at the Rent Tribunal, the chairman is legally qualified, whereas this is not generally the case at SBATs. Furthermore
one member of the Rent Tribunal (the valuer) is selected specifically for his professional expertise whereas at SBATs it is claimed
that members are selected on the basis of more abstract qualifications (such as knowledge of the local community). The interaction
between different types of representative, and different types of
chairmen and members (legally qualified, professionally qualified
or lay) constitute an important variable. On the basis of our
initial observations at these two types of tribunal, it was decided
that a more specialised project should take into account the re-
ciprocal images and expectations held by these two groups. The
'effect' of representation might then be viewed in two ways: first,

the short-term effect of the outcome of the hearing for individual appellants; second, the long-term effect on the decision-making process of the tribunal itself.

Representation must also be viewed in relation to the function of each tribunal. Rent Tribunals and SBATs provide examples of contrasting functions. SBATs are concerned with mediating between an individual and a government department, and in this, they are typical of many tribunals. Rent Tribunals perform the more unusual function of mediating in disputes between individuals, i.e. landlord and tenant. Observations suggested that this contrast in functions also permitted differing degrees of autonomy, with Rent Tribunals exhibiting far greater autonomy. At hearings of this tribunal, the Department of the Environment is far removed from the issues in dispute. No departmental view is presented at hearings, and the clerk to the tribunal, as we shall show, tends to perform duties which are solely administrative in nature. This situation contrasts strongly with that prevailing at SBATs, which by their very function are closely related to a government department (DHSS). Supplementary Benefit Commission policy is very much in evidence at SBAT hearings as the Presenting Officer attends as the Commission's representative and the clerk, too, plays a more active role.

The differing functions of these two tribunals, in terms of whether or not a government department is involved in the dispute to be mediated, suggests the importance of viewing representation in the context of the independence of tribunals from their relevant government departments. In considering independence, we were concerned to take into account both the position as laid down in statute and also the reality of day-to-day practice at tribunals. Apart from considering the independence of tribunals in relation to the function they perform, a study of Rent Tribunals and SBATs also provides a useful opportunity of viewing independence through contrasting structures. These two tribunals differ in the way they are constituted, Rent Tribunals being based on a presidential system. This too, lends to those tribunals greater autonomy. (1)

When the Franks Committee reviewed the position and workings of tribunals, one of their advantages over the courts was said to be their 'freedom from technicality'. (2) This is not, however, a uniform quality. Observations suggested to us that differences derived from the legislation governing their decision-making, from the intervention of policy considerations and from the presence or absence of specialist opinion on the tribunal itself. 'Freedom from technicality' and the related issue of the degree of discretion available to tribunals also need to be treated as variables. We suspected, too, that the appropriateness of different styles of representation might vary according to the tribunal itself, and according to the features of the tribunal which added together provide some measure of 'technicality'. It appeared, however, that SBATs and Rent Tribunals did not provide a sufficient contrast in this respect. Whilst SBATs show a far greater use of discretion in decision-making, Rent Tribunals do not go to the other extreme of relying heavily on precedent. We decided therefore that our study of administrative tribunals could usefully be expanded by including National Insurance Local Tribunals (NILTs) where the use of discretion is reduced by heavy reliance on statute and case law and on precedent.

The three types of tribunal chosen provide then a diversity of variables of importance when considering the question of representation: first, the presence or absence of legally qualified chairmen and professional or lay members. Second, the function of tribunals in terms of whether or not they are arbitrating between individuals or between an individual and a government department and the related issue of independence; third, the use of discretion or precedent in decision-making.

CHOICE OF AREAS

Since the project employed two research workers, it was decided that the fieldwork should be divided evenly between two areas of the country. That London should be one of those areas was a foregone conclusion, for reasons of finance, administration and convenience. But whilst this study cannot pretend to reflect the national situation we were anxious that it should not be confined to London where the atypical nature of government offices (with a rapid staff turnover and a large number of claimants), as well as the acute housing situation, would be reflected in the appeals procedure, thereby producing a one-sided view.

The choice of a second city was based on a number of criteria. First, we were interested in the level of local unemployment since this would affect the workload of both NILTs and SBATs. Second, the size of the private furnished accommodation market was considered (and this provided something of a problem, since many cities outside London have a relatively small proportion of furnished accommodation). The level of local community and trade union organisation was also taken into consideration, in the hope that this would be reflected in the incidence of representation at local tribunals. This factor was important because our interest in the effects of representation made it desirable to choose an area where at least an appreciable measure of representation at tribunals took place. (As we have pointed out this study is not concerned so much with how little or how much representation occurs, but rather the effects of it when it does occur.) Finally, we paid some attention to the rural-urban fringe of each city under consideration. This was relevant because we wished to include, for the two areas in the study, inner-city, suburban and outer-city tribunals. The last category was to include tribunals serving some rural areas. In these different locations, the type of problems occurring at tribunals vary (depending on demographic, industrial and housing conditions). Furthermore, certain types of representation are more a feature of inner-city areas, related to community-group organisation. By including suburban and outer-city tribunals, we hoped to present a more complete picture of the occurrence of representation.

The second major city selected for study, located in the north west both measured up to the above criteria, and had the added advantage of falling within discreet administrative areas for the three types of tribunal in the study, a situation which simplified the task of obtaining relevant statistics.

The selection of individual local tribunals within the two regions was also based on several considerations. In London, it was

felt that the fieldwork should be carried out 'south of the river'
(a neglected area as far as research is concerned). Beyond that, the
choice of tribunals depended on an examination of the statistics of
local tribunals (related to workload, type of case and where available, the level of representation). In the case of NILTs and SBATs,
the choice also depended to some extent on advice offered by
officials of DHSS. They suggested that certain tribunals were unsuitable for study, generally because there was no chairman at that
time (owing to death or illness) or that two tribunals were about to
be amalgamated and to include only one would produce administrative
difficulties.

London South (the DHSS Administrative area covering south London
and extending to the coast) covers 10 SBATs and 17 NILTs. One inner-
London area provided examples of both a SBAT and a NILT, and two
suburban and two south-coast towns were choosen for the study of
suburban and outer areas. The Rent Tribunals were chosen to cover,
where possible, comparable areas. The inner-city and suburban
tribunals are administered by the London Rent Assessment Panel, the
outer tribunal by the Sussex Rent Assessment Panel.

In the second area studied, the DHSS region, north-west Merseyside
covers 9 SBATs and 14 NILTs. Again, tribunals were selected to
exemplify inner-city, suburban and more rural locations. The selection of Rent Tribunals differed slightly from the south, since one
Rent Assessment Panel covers the entire area, with tribunals sitting
in various locations within the region as the need arises. Rent
Tribunals were selected to cover the same areas as SBATs and NILTs.

The two regions in the south and north-west show some marked
differences in terms of industry, employment and housing. Whilst it
is beyond the scope of this study to present any detailed description
of the two areas, an outline of the social and economic background
against which the study was conducted may assist the reader in the
interpretation of subsequent findings.

LIVERPOOL AND SOUTH LONDON — THE BACKGROUND TO OUR STUDY

For the past fifty years, Merseyside has been regarded as one of
Britain's problem areas. Despite national and local measures of
assistance and the development of industrial estates such as Speke
and Kirkby, unemployment (particularly amongst unskilled labour) remains higher than the national average. Whilst throughout the north-
west the unemployment rate tends to be higher than the national
average, that for the region as a whole is only about a half of the
rate for Merseyside itself. Tribunal members in the outer areas
often commented that 'anyone can get work if he wants it'. (3)

On Merseyside itself tradional jobs have been lost following the
modernisation of the docks and the contraction of related industries
such as ship-building and repairing. The giant car plants on the
periphery of the area have not compensated totally for the loss.

St Helens is dominated by the giant glass-making firm of
Pilkingtons, although the mines still provide a source of employment.
Also located in the region are Widnes and Runcorn New Town, where
many re-housed Liverpudlians live and here heavy industry is located,
predominantly chemical manufacturing processes.

The outer area of the north-west region encompasses market towns and rural areas which have attracted a substantial tourist industry. However, it also includes the heart of the chemical industry dominated by ICI

The inner-city area selected for study in south London, is an area of poor housing, relatively high unemployment and with a substantial immigrant population. (Our observations at tribunals in this area showed that a quarter of appellants were non-white, compared with only 4 per cent in the north west.) Employment reflects the demands of an inner-city area, with an emphasis on services and light industry.

The south London suburbs selected for study spread across a fairly wide area and are far less homogeneous than their counterparts in the north west, although one town included is an industrial town with extensive engineering and chemical works.

The outer area for this part of the project extended to the south coast. The coastal towns selected are characterised by lack of industry, a seasonal tourist industry and a high proportion of retired people. Cases observed at tribunals in this area (although constituting a small proportion of the toal cases in the sample) reflected the weighted age structure of the population, with an emphasis on those over 65.

One of the most striking differences between the two regions relates to patterns of housing tenure. In the north west, the re-development of inner-city areas together with the Corporation's tradition of providing council housing has resulted in a situation where about 40 per cent of all housing is owned by the Corporation. (4)

In the suburban area studied the proportion of council housing is over 30 per cent and in this part of the country, the furnished accommodation market is relatively small. In the inner-city, only 4 per cent of all tenure is rented furnished accommodation and in the suburban area only 1 per cent. This contrasts strongly with our inner-London area, where the furnished rented sector accounts for 15 per cent of all tenures and even one south-coast town where the figure is 10 per cent. Differences between the two regions were also reflected in our observations at Rent Tribunals. In the southern tribunals the issue of security was prevalent whereas in the north west concern over the level of rents was often the foremost factor.

Analysis of interviews with appellants and also of our observations reflects some of the regional differences described above. At NILTs, a higher proportion of unemployment cases and those arising from industrial injury occurred in the north west. Tribunals in this region also heard more cases arising from trades disputes, following lay-offs at car plants and also during the miners' strike.

The pattern and tradition of industry in the north west is also indicated by the role of organised labour. In our sample from this region, 48 per cent of appellants belonged to trade unions, compared with 19 per cent in south London, and more appellants consulted a trade union before appearing at a NILT in the north west than did appellants in south London. Up to 30 per cent of represented cases observed at NILTs in the north west were conducted by trade union officials, compared with 10 per cent of represented cases in south London.

Interviews with people who had represented cases at tribunals also
reflected regional differences. Our sample of interviewees in the
north west contained a higher proportion of trade union officials,
generally officers who specialised in this type of work and who belonged to larger unions such as NUM, TGWU, GMWU and AUEW. Unlike
south London, where we interviewed representatives from a wide
range of helping agencies, much of the voluntary work relating to
tribunal hearings in the north-western city is carried out by
CHECK!, an agency specialising in giving advice and representation.
The concentration of this type of work on one agency is reflected in
our findings, where one quarter of all representatives interviewed in
this area were from CHECK!

METHOD OF STUDY

Access

Initial meetings between LARU and officials of the London headquarters of DHSS took place at the end of 1972 whilst the research
design was being formulated. Fieldwork was expected to last 9
months, divided into equal periods spent with the three types of
tribunal. At that stage geographical areas had not been selected for
the study, and statistical data were required from DHSS in order to
make the choice. We had decided that our primary data would be from
four different sources: (i) observations at tribunal hearings; (ii)
interviews with appellants; (iii) interviews with chairmen and
members; (iv) interviews with representatives.

When we approached DHSS with a request for statistical information, we were not prepared for the complicated and protracted
negotiations which were to follow. This is not to say that our wish
to do research was hindered or blocked by the Department in any way;
but rather that their concern to give us official backing and their
desire that we should obtain a good response from the tribunals, led
to fairly complicated procedural arrangements.

In the first place, obtaining relevant statistics was not a
straightforward task. Apart from the minimum national statistics
which are published, more detailed national figures and all regional
figures involved DHSS in providing specially produced computer
tables. No regional statistics on representation were available for
NILTs in the London area, and local statistics for all the tribunals
had to be collated manually by the research team.

We mentioned earlier that at the time of our study, staff at local
DHSS offices were involved in an industrial dispute. Officials at
headquarters were most concerned that our research would not put
unacceptable pressure on local offices, and we had to assure them
that our project was relatively small in scale, and that all data
collection could be done by our own workers. With these assurances,
headquarters of DHSS approached the relevant regional staff and
facilitated our access to their offices and staff. Even with this
help, the time lapse between our first contact with officials, and
the date of starting fieldwork was considerable (six months).

Part of the reason for this delay concerned the problem of gaining
access to potential interviewees. This was not true in relation to

chairmen and members of tribunals; in their case, DHSS decided that
it would be best for the Department to write to all the chairmen
and members of NILTs and SBATs of the relevant tribunals (once
chosen) telling them briefly about the nature of the research, and
warning them that they might see a research worker at tribunal hearings and be asked to give an interview. This proved to be very helpful, since it both lent offical blessing to our research and stressed
our independent status, making subsequent contacts with tribunal
chairmen and members far easier.

The problems arose in contacting appellants and representatives.
Since we wished to draw samples from cases already heard (rather than
contacting interviewees as they emerged from hearings) this intro-
duced problems of confidentiality for DHSS, particularly after the
Younger Committee's report on privacy. Eventually a complicated
system of contacting appellants and representatives was drawn up,
with DHSS approaching interviewees on LARU's behalf, and replies
being sent direct to LARU. Two considerations guided the procedure;
that potential interviewees should appreciate that the project was
independent and not sponsored by DHSS; and that DHSS should feel
that they had preserved confidentiality until interviewees consented
to take part in our study. (5) Given its complexities the system
worked well, but did involve some delay between drawing the sample
and conducting the interviews.

Our experience in gaining access to Rent Tribunals was quite
different. One brief meeting with an official of the Department of
the Environment informed us that the Department would not be concerned with negotiations for access. We were told to contact the
presidents of the Rent Assessment Panels (from whom tribunal chairmen and members are drawn) in the relevant areas. This provided
another example of the relative autonomy of Rent Tribunals compared
with that of NILTs and SBATs, but the absence of what amounted to
an official 'blessing' provided us with some problems of access to.
Rent Tribunals.

We needed the agreement of three presidents (one for the north
west, two for the southern area). In two cases this was forthcoming,
the third, London, presented considerable difficulties. The president
felt that the views of members concerning legal representation at
tribunals, and the extension of legal aid, had been stated fully in
their memorandum to the Legal Aid Advisory Committee. The president
seemed unwilling for research workers to interview tribunal chairmen
and members individually, and offered to make provisions for group
interviews to take place at the headquarters of the London Rent
Assessment Panel. This was not acceptable to us, and the subsequent
response rate of chairmen and members of Rent Tribunals in the
London area was adversely affected. (This is discussed more fully
below.) At the inner-London Rent Tribunal selected for study, the
chairmen and members would only consent to a group discussion and
furthermore the research worker was not allowed to draw a sample of
applicants from tribunal papers, but had to make arrangements for
interviews after each hearing. At the suburban tribunal in
London, no interviews with the chairmen or members took place,
although access to papers was given so that a proper sample of
applicants could be drawn.

Sampling

Some reference has already been made to the way in which appellants
were selected for interview. A more detailed description of the
sampling of the three groups of interviewees is given here.
   In the case of tribunal chairmen, we attempted to interview as
many as possible since pilot interviews during the first year's work
had indicated that chairmen were likely to play a prominant role in a
tribunal's procedure and decision-making. Their views, therefore,
were of particular interest to us. The names of tribunal members
whom we wished to interview were drawn randomly according to panel
(i.e. equal numbers of employers' and employees' members for NILTs;
ministers members and other members for SBATS; valuers and lay
members for Rent Tribunals). The number of members selected for
interview at each tribunal was determined by the relative size of
the tribunal's membership
   Samples of appellants and representatives were, where possible,
drawn from appeal documents but the latter sample was augmented by
research workers contacting representatives after hearings, or
through local organisations. When names of representatives were
drawn from appeal documents certain categories were excluded. These
were close relatives or some other person who, as far as the research
worker could determine had 'accompanied' the appellant rather than
'represented' him at the hearing.
   In sampling appellants, two main factors were taken into account.
First, the time period over which cases were drawn. A balance had
to be struck between a sufficiently long period to enable enough
cases to be drawn, and a period short enough to permit reasonable
recall by appellants of events and attitudes. Second, we attempted
to sample equal numbers of represented and non-represented cases for
interview, but at certain tribunals and in certain areas this was
impossible, since there were too few represented cases.
   We found it necessary to augment our sample of appellants by
using 'reserve lists' of potential interviewees, drawn in the same
way as the original sample. Since our proposed sample of appellants
was only 300 cases (100 for each type of tribunal) we could not
afford a high non-response rate; this would have created difficulties at the analysis stage. We therefore decided to substitute
cases in an effort to maintain our proposed sample size, at the
same time attempting not to reinforce the non-reponse bias by
compiling the reserve list according to the same principles as the
original list and by maintaining the balance of cases as outlined
above. Access to carry out this study was, for the most part,
readily given and the London Rent Tribunals provided the only exception to the full co-operation.

TABLE 2.1   Comparison of proposed and actual sample sizes (6)

Sample	Chairmen and members	Representatives	Appellants	Total
Proposed sample	150	150	300	600
Actual sample	115	103	229	446

Amongst chairmen and members of tribunals, the response rate was generally good. In the case of NILTs and SBATs, this was certainly facilitated by the initial introductory letters sent out by DHSS. At Rent Tribunals, the poor reponse was confined to London, as we have mentioned, where one tribunal completely refused any form of interview and where another would only permit a group discussion.

The response rates for representatives at SBATs and NILTs was 68 per cent, and at Rent Tribunals 71 per cent. Only 5 per cent of the sample refused to be interviewed, the reason given by several being that as they had only acted as a representative once, they did not feel qualified to answer more general questions about tribunals. It seems likely that the non-response amongst representatives was partly caused by difficulties in tracing them from the information included on appeal documents.

Amongst appellants, it is important to consider the reponse rate for Rent Tribunals separately from the other two types of tribunal. This is partly because the samples were contacted differently, but more importantly one must consider the significance of requests for interview being returned marked 'gone away'. With appellants at NILTs and SBATs, this would indicate that these appellants were 'units outside the population' and hence could be subtracted from the sample size before calculating a response rate. (7) At Rent Tribunals, where the issue of security of tenure is involved, a letter

TABLE 2.2 Response rates of appellants at SBATs and NILTs

Reply	Initial sample (%)	Initial sample + reserve lists (%)
Response	53	46
Refusal	9	7
	} 47	} 54
Non-response	38	47
Total	100	100

TABLE 2.3 Response rates of applicants at Rent Tribunals

Reply	North west (%)	South London (%)
Response	26	25
Refusal	0	6
Returned 'gone away'	22	*
Non-response	52	*
		} 69
Total	100	100

* These cells cannot be filled in for the south, since applicants were contacted by different methods.

returned marked 'gone away' has more significance; too many non-respondents in this category could obviously introduce bias. Tables 2.2 and 2.3 show that the response rates were somewhat disappointing, particularly at Rent Tribunals. It is important to repeat, however, that in order to obtain a sufficiently large sample for analysis extra letters were sent out to potential interviewees on our reserve lists after the initial non-response was known.

The most frequent reason for refusing interview was that the appellant 'didn't know anything about tribunals'. Others gave as reasons illness, only wanting to give information by post, and so on. One man was in the process of contacting his MP about his case and did not feel it would be right to be interviewed.

Amongst appellants at SBATs and NILTs, (8) there were slightly higher non-response and refusal rates in the south. A higher proportion of those non-reponding failed to attend the tribunal hearing (46 per cent compared with 20 per cent of those interviewed). There was no significant difference between respondents and non-respondents in terms of the type of case, or in terms of the outcome of the hearing. These last two factors seemed to us to be important when considering whether those appellants interviewed constituted a biased sample. We feel that the appellants in this sample constitute a relatively typical group of represented and non-represented appellants from these two areas of the country.

A disturbing feature of those who did agree to be interviewed was the number of appellants who were judged by the research workers to be in obvious need, particularly among non-attenders. (9) It appeared to the research workers that some, at least, looked upon the interview as a last hope, and the workers were often asked 'can you do anything?'

Observations and interviews

The primary data collected were of two different types, derived from observations and interviews. On at least one day each week a research worker attended a session of the tribunal currently being studied. For each case heard during that session, an observation schedule was filled in. The schedule was divided into two parts: the first consisted of precoded categories and enabled the research worker to fill in the basic details of each case; these categories included the type of case, the outcome of the hearing, details of attendance and representation and so on. The second part of the schedule was left 'open', that is, the information recorded was based entirely on the research worker's observations, guided only by a check-list of all the people likely to be present at the hearing (tribunal chairman, members drawn from different panels, government official, appellant, representative, clerk). Against this list the research worker noted the type of role played by each, whether dominant or minor, the type of arguments employed, the way a case was presented by an appellant or a representative and the response of the tribunal. The research workers based in the different regions held discussions and read each other's work in order to improve consistency in the way these schedules were completed.

Interviews were conducted with three groups of people involved in

tribunal hearings; chairmen and members, appellants and representatives. For the most part the interview schedules consisted of
'open' questions, that is they permitted interviewees to reply at
some length if they wished, and their responses were recorded verbatim as far as possible. In effect, we were attempting to conduct
the interview as though it were a structured conversation. Experience during the Unit's early fieldwork had convinced us that when
asking questions which are complicated, or which the interviewee
may never have previously considered, it was important to provide the
person with the time to 'think aloud' and so present a considered
response. Through these interviews we were attempting to discern
the perspectives of three different groups of people, drawn together
by the experience of tribunal hearings. Many of the questions,
particularly those asked of chairmen, members and representatives,
were the same. These were not concerned with the cases of particular appellants but with how the interviewee came to be involved
with tribunals, how they saw their own contribution to a hearing as
well as that of other participants, the relevance of their own personal expertise and experiences, views about policy matters and
tribunals generally, and questions concerned with representation and
related issues. Many of the questions were complex and some respondents found them difficult to answer; in some cases we were
asking interviewees to talk about abstract subjects which might not
previously have been covered in conversation.

The appellants interviewed were not the same as those observed at
hearings. Since we wished to obtain a fairly equal distribution of
represented and non-represented cases a sample had to be drawn in
advance. Furthermore it would have been disruptive at hearings had
the research worker attempted to contact appellants for interview
as well as making observations of the hearing. The research
workers, therefore, were not familiar with the details of the cases
of those appellants who were interviewed and part of each interview
was devoted to listening to the details of the appellant's case as
he saw it, and his experience at the tribunal. As with the tribunal
personnel and representatives, however, we were also trying to build
up a picture of how appellants saw the tribunal situation, how
appropriate they felt it to be to their experience and problems, how
they managed at the hearing and so on.

In addition to the unstructured material in the interviews, each
group was asked a comparable set of questions which were straightforward and factual, relating to their personal histories (age,
occupation, education and similar details). This material provided
us with a basis from which to construct a description of the three
groups interviewed.

The interviews were generally carried out at respondents' homes
after making an appointment. Some chairmen, members and representatives were interviewed at their offices and the occasional interview
was conducted at a cafe or pub. (10) The interviews generally
lasted between one and two hours, some were slightly longer. This
contrasted strongly with the observations at tribunal hearings,
where cases were for the most part dealt with briefly (particularly
if not attended by the appellant) although the Rent Tribunal did
provide an important exception. This is discussed more fully in
chapter 6.

Analysis

The main problem concerning analysis related to the best way of
using the valuable responses obtained in 'open' questions on the
interview schedules. Since they could not be used in their entirety,
some degree of generalisation was essential. The information was
condensed by coding it into more general categories, such categories
being arrived at by selecting a random sample of responses to a given
question, copying out all the responses verbatim and then inspecting
them and sorting them into patterns of answers. Answers which could
not be categorised were recorded separately. The system evolved for
coding allowed us to record several answers given by one respondent
to one question and in the analysis given later, some responses are
not exclusive.

   Coding the data took five weeks, and was carried out by two research workers helped by two graduates employed specifically for
that task. Data were transferred from the interview schedules to
transfer sheets and then to punched cards. These were analysed by
computer at the University of London Computer Centre.

STUDY SAMPLES AND OBSERVATIONS

A total of 229 appellants were interviewed, evenly distributed between south London and the north west (50.7 per cent and 49.3 per
cent respectively). Table 2.4 shows the numbers interviewed in each
locality, according to the type of tribunal to which they had
applied. Appellants to NILTs and SBATs form the major part of the
sample (41 per cent and 41.9 per cent respectively); less than one
fifth of the sample had applied to the Rent Tribunal (a result of
cutting short the fieldwork).

TABLE 2.4 The sample of appellants according to type of tribunal
and location

Area	NILT N	SBAT N	RT N	Total N
South London				
Inner	26	26	4	56
Suburban	12	14	9	35
Outer	10	6	9	25
North west				
Inner	35	34	17	86
Suburban	7	9	0	16
Outer	4	7	0	11
Total	94 (41%)	96 (41.9%)	39 (17%)	229 (100%)

   Amongst the 115 tribunal chairmen and members interviewed, 17
were legally qualified chairmen, 12 were chairmen without a legal
background and a further 3 were reserve chairmen. This reflects the
weighting we had decided to accord to the views of tribunal chairmen.
The remaining 83 in the sample were tribunal members, drawn in equal

proportions from the various panels which made up the tribunals.
Just over half of these interviews were conducted in the north-west
area (52 per cent), the rest in London and the south. As with the
sample of appellants, the majority of these interviewees were from
NILTs and SBATs (44.3 per cent and 42.6 per cent - see Table 2.5).
Only 13 per cent of the sample were from Rent Tribunals owing to a
combination of the high refusal rate and the attenuated fieldwork.
In addition to the Rent Tribunal interviews, however, information derived from a group discussion with Rent Tribunal members in inner
London is incorporated into the main body of findings even though it
cannot be used statistically.

TABLE 2.5 The sample of tribunal chairmen and members according to
type of tribunal and location

Area	NILT N	SBAT N	RT N	Total N
South London				
Inner	13	12	0	25
Suburban	6	8	0	14
Outer	6	4	6	16
North west				
Inner	17	14	9	40
Suburban	6	4	0	10
Outer	3	7	0	10
Total	51 (44.3%)	49 (42.6%)	15 (13%)	115 (100%)

The sample of representatives numbered 103, again evenly distributed between the North west and London areas (51.5 per cent and
48.5 per cent respectively). As with the other samples, the proportion of representatives from Rent Tribunals is low (see Table 2.6).
One third of the representatives had some form of legal background
(a small proportion were still studying).

TABLE 2.6 The sample of representatives at tribunals according to
type of tribunal and location

Area	NILT N	SBAT N	RT N	Total N
South London				
Inner	8	12	1	21
Suburban	7	7	5	19
Outer	2	2	6	10
North west				
Inner	19	16	5	40
Suburban	6	3	0	9
Outer	1	3	0	4
Total	43 (41.7%)	43 (41.7%)	17 (16.5%)	103 (100%)

Finally, the data include information from observations at tribunal hearings. Sixty-five sessions were attended by research workers, producing a total of 276 observed cases. Table 2.7 shows the distribution of observed cases according to the type of tribunal and the region of the country.

TABLE 2.7   Observed cases at tribunal hearings, according to type of tribunal and region

Area	NILT N	SBAT N	RT N	Total N
South London	45	57	45	147
North west	56	56	17·	129
Total	101 (36.5%)	113 (41%)	62 (22.5%)·	276 (100%)

SOCIAL CHARACTERISTICS OF THE RESPONDENTS (11)

A comparison of certain social characteristics of the groups interviewed produce some interesting contrasts. The differences between tribunal chairmen and members, and the appellants who appear before them, is perhaps predictable and is indicative of the social distance existing between these two groups. The characteristics of representatives, on the other hand, suggests a third quite distinct group of people; they were similar to chairmen and members in terms of social class and educational background, but very different in terms of age and attitudes.

The chairmen and members interviewed were a markedly older group than the appellants. Only a very small proportion of the former were under 35 (1.7 per cent) compared with appellants (34 per cent). Over half the chairmen and members were older than 60 compared with only 20 per cent of appellants. Representatives tended to be a very young group, nearly half being under 35 (Table 2.8).

TABLE 2.8   Age of the respondents*

Age	Chairmen and members %	Appellants %	Representatives %
Under 35	1.7	34.0	49.5
35 - under 60	44.3	46.3	39.6
60 or over	53.9	19.7	10.9
Total	100 (N=115)	100 (N=229)	100 (N=101)

* Totals may not agree with sample size as cases where there is no information are excluded.

Tribunal chairmen and members generally belonged to a higher social class than appellants. (12) Nearly three quarters of the former were in RG categories I or II (professional, managerial, intermediate occupations), compared with I7 per cent of appellants. Over 40 per cent of appellants were from classes comprising semi-skilled or unskilled workers. Representatives showed far more similarity to chairmen and members in terms of social class than they did to appellants (Table 2.9).

TABLE 2.9   Social class of repondents as indicated by Registrar-General's categories*

RG Category	Chairmen and members %	Appellants %	Representatives %
I and II	74.6	16.8	81.3
III	21.9	35.4	7.8
IV and V	3.5	41.1	3.9
Other (mainly students)	0	6.2	6.9
Total	100 (N=114)	100 (N=225)	100 (N=102)

* Totals may not agree with sample size as cases where there is no information are excluded.

In terms of educational and professional qualifications, chairmen and members stood in marked contrast to appellants, over a third of the latter having left school by the age of 15. Representatives were a very highly qualified group, over half having either a degree, a professional qualification or both, and the remainder some technical skill or expertise (see Table 2.10).

TABLE 2.10   Educational or professional qualifications of respondents*

Qualification	Chairmen and members %	Appellants %	Representatives %
Professional or degree	31.3	6.6	57.5
Other	35.7	34.4	25.7
None	33.0	58.8	16.8
Total	100 (N=115)	100 (N=226)	100 (N=101)

* Totals may not agree with sample size as cases where there is no information are excluded.

Questions relating to income were only asked of appellants and repesentatives. On DHSS advice, this question was excluded from the tribunal chairmen and members' interview schedule. (The good

response rate from the two groups asked suggest that sensitivity
was not very great.) A high proportion of appellants had an income
of less than £20 per week, and even amongst representatives, almost
one quarter were in this category (Table 2.11). The reasons differed
however: the low income of appellants was due to the fact that, for
many, welfare benefits were their only source of income. In the
case of representatives, it was generally due to their youthfulness
and to the fact that they were at the beginning of their career.
Over 70 per cent of appellants said their income was insufficient to
meet their needs. Whilst data on income is not available for members
and chairmen, given known factors about them such as social class,
qualifications, age (and therefore experience), it is reasonable to
hypothesise that on this factor too, they stand in marked contrast to
appellants.

TABLE 2.11   Income of respondents*

Income	Chairmen and members %	Appellants %	Representatives %
Under £20 per week		41.7	23
£20-under £40 per week	Not asked	43.6	25
£40 or more		12.9	50
Unwilling to disclose		1.8	2
Total		100 (N=225)	100 (N=100)

* Totals may not agree with sample sizes as cases where there is no
  information are excluded.

   To summarise, our respondents form three distinct groups in terms
of the factors discussed. The chairmen and members of tribunals tend
to be in the older age groups, of high social class and generally
well qualified. Appellants are somewhat younger, of lower social
class, poorly qualified and many are very poor. Representatives
appear to be a young, very highly qualified group; a great many are
of high social class but their incomes tend not to reflect this.

STATISTICAL COMPARISONS

In this section, data derived from our observations at tribunal hearings are compared with statistics from other sources in an attempt
to assess how representative are our findings. (13) The section
deals first with observations at NILTs and SBATs, since these form
the major part of the data.
   Obtaining statistics about NILTs and SBATs with which to compare
our data presented a problem, since only a bare minimum (relating to
appeals nationally) are published.

The incidence of regional variations in the proportion of appeals allowed at tribunals reduces the value of using national statistics for this purpose. (14) Furthermore, until recently no statistics re- lating to representation have been routinely collected by DHSS, although this is now carried out for SBATs on a national basis but not on a regional basis. No statistics were available for the selected local tribunals in the study, so research workers collated these from papers in local DHSS offices. Finally, of course, data were derived from our observations of cases at tribunal hearings. Two drawbacks are attached to the comparative use of these figures. In the first place, data from different sources are based on different time periods; this was unavoidable if any statistics were to be obtained at all. Second, there were problems of definition when deciding whether some cases we had observed had in fact been 'allowed' at the hearing. At NILTs, for example, an appeal relating to unemployment benefit may be disallowed but the period of dis- qualification from benefit may be reduced. At SBATs, an appellant may not be allowed all that he asked for but might be given part of it (or even a payment for something quite different). Following definitions employed by DHSS, appeals at NILTs were only classified as 'allowed' if they were allowed completely (the existence of a second level of appeal to the Commissioner leaves the appellant with the opportunity of appealing against all other decisions, even compro- mises). At SBATs, the reverse is the case, in that tribunal decisions are defined as revised decisions if there is any increase in benefit, or any single payment is to be made, regardless of what the appellant was actually claiming.

Table 2.12 compares the proportion of appeals allowed at NILTs in

TABLE 2.12   National Insurance Local Tribunals: appeals allowed – comparative statistics

Area	Source	Time period	Total cases	% allowed
North West (Merseyside)	DHSS computer print-out	July 1972– June 1973	3,083	21.2
3 study NILTs	Compiled by LARU at local DHSS offices	January– December 1972	1,238	17.6
3 study NILTs	Observations at hearings	November 1973– January 1974	56	16.1
London South	DHSS computer print-out	July 1972– June 1973	2,640	19.9
3 study NILTs	Compiled by LARU at local DHSS offices	January– December 1972	813	16.6
3 study NILTs	Observations at hearings	June– October 1973	45	13.3
National	DHSS Annual Report 1973	1973	29,477	20

the two study regions. It shows that in the regions taken as a
whole, the proportion of appeals allowed reflects the national
average (north west (Merseyside) 21.2 per cent; London South 19.9
per cent; National 20 per cent). Background statistics collected
by the research team about the tribunals selected for study indicate
that in the year preceding the fieldwork, these tribunals allowed a
somewhat smaller proportion of appeals than was the case for each
region taken in its entirety (north-west study NILTs 17.6 per cent;
London South study NILTs 16.6 per cent). During the fieldwork period
itself, the proportion of appeals allowed at NILTs in each region was
still lower (north-west study NILTs 16.1 per cent; London South
study NILTs 13.3 per cent).

The picture that emerges of the observations at NILTs, therefore,
is that these particular tribunals allowed a smaller proportion of
appeals than the regional averages, and also a smaller proportion
than they themselves had allowed in a prior twelve-month period.
(The reservations mentioned above, relating to time period and definitions, must apply and also the relatively small size of the observation sample.)

Table 2.13 shows that the situation is completely different with
SBATs. The north-west (Merseyside) region revised far fewer decisions
in the appellants' favour (9.8 per cent, compared with 17.4 per cent

TABLE 2.13 Supplementary Benefit Appeal Tribunals: decisions in
appellant's favour - comparative statistics

Area	Source	Time period	Total cases	% revised
North west (Merseyside)	DHSS computer print-out	October 1972 March 1972	1,415	9.8
3 study SBATs	Compiled by LARU at local DHSS offices	January- December 1972	1,841	7.4
3 study SBATs	Observations at hearings	January- March 1974	56	28.6
London South	DHSS computer print-out	October 1972- March 1973	1,262	17.4
3 study SBATs	Compiled by LARU at local DHSS offices	January- December 1972	942	11.5
3 study SBATs	Observations at hearings	December 1973- March 1974	57	21
National	DHSS Annual Report 1973	1973	26,002	19

in London South; 19 per cent nationally). Statistics relating to
the SBATs chosen for study show that in the year prior to our research, these tribunals revised a smaller proportion of appeals than
their regional averages (north-west study SBATs 7.4 per cent;
London South study SBATs 11.5 per cent) but at our observations at

these SBATs, an unusually high proportion of appeals were allowed
(north west 28.6 per cent; London South 21 per cent). Once again,
the different time priods on which these figures are based may be
important. There may have been a 'liberalising' trend in the inter-
vening period. Furthermore, we are not entirely satisfied at the
consistency of definition of a 'revised decision' when a compromise is
made, either by us when recording observations, or by the clerks.
Our interpretation of DHSS definitions may be too liberal.

We have no reason to suppose that the cases observed were atypical - they were not selected in any way except by date of hearing.
An explanation that cannot be ignored is that there was a change in
the tribunals' decision-making simply because a research worker was
present. This is not uncommon in research situations. (15) The
amount of discretion available to SBATs makes it more likely that any
effect of being observed will be manifested here rather than at
NILTs.

Our observations at NILTs recorded that 42.6 per cent of appellants attended the hearing of the case, which reflects the national
rate of attendance (46.3 per cent during April 1971 - March 1972).
At SBATs, however, our observations showed a somewhat higher
attendance rate (54.8 per cent, compared with a national rate of
43 per cent during the period October 1972 - March 1973). Whilst
this higher attendance rate may account in part for the higher
success rate of appeals noted above, it does not seem likely that
this factor alone provides a sufficient explanation, since the
difference in 'success' rates is far greater than the difference in
attendance rates.

As we mentioned at the beginning of this section, reliable data
about appellants who were represented at tribunals are difficult to
obtain. Data from DHSS suggest that 20 per cent of appellants are
represented at SBATs, but this figure makes no distinction between
appellants who are merely accompanied by a friend or relative and
those who are represented by the same. (This same data suggest that
two thirds of the representation at SBATs is carried out by friends
and relatives of appellants.) Our own observation data only included as representatives those who played an active role at the
hearing as opposed to a purely supportive one. We found that 17.9
per cent of appellants were represented at NILTs, 18.5 per cent
at SBATs.

TABLE 2.14 National statistics on attendance and representation at
SBATs, related to outcome of appeal

Appellants	Number of cases	% decisions in appellant's favour
Attended and represented	2,315	37
Attended and not represented	3,969	25
Not attended but represented	614	32
Not attended and not represented	7,647	6

Source: DHSS computer print-out for October 1972 - March 1973.

National statistics indicate that at SBATs, attendance of the
appellant and representation are important variables when considering the proportion of appeals decided in the appellants' favour.
Table 2.14 shows that the success rates for appeals ranged from 6
per cent for those who neither attended nor were represented, to 37
per cent for those who attended and were also represented. Even
when the appellant did not attend but was represented in his absence,
32 per cent were decided in the appellant's favour. Our own observations at hearings of both SBATs and NILTs reflect this tendency,
particularly the great contrast in the outcome for attended and non-
attended cases. (16) (See Tables 2.15 and 2.16. Unfortunately the
number of represented cases is small in these cross-tabulations, and
percentages which are bracketed must be regarded with caution.)

TABLE 2.15   Attendance and representation at observed NILTs related
to outcome of appeal

Appellants	Number of cases	% appeals allowed
Attended and represented	13	[23.1]
Attended and not represented	30	26.7
Not attended but represented	0	[-]
Not attended and not represented	53	7.5

TABLE 2.16   Attendance and representation at observed SBATs related
to outcome of appeal

Appellants	Number of cases	% revised decisions
Attended and represented	17	41.2
Attended and not represented	45	40.0
Not attended but represented	4	[25.0]
Not attended and not represented	46	4.4

Observations at Rent Tribunals comprised a minor part of the
fieldwork, and since only 62 cases were observed it is not possible
to present detailed statistical breakdowns. Attendance by tenants
at hearings was extremely high, 85.5 per cent, and contrasts
strongly with attendance of appellants at NILTs and SBATs. 14.5 per
cent of tenants were represented at hearings (compared with 39 per
cent of landlords). The majority of applications (75.8 per cent)
were concerned with security. Amongst the 62 cases, some security
of tenure was granted to 78.9 per cent. In one third of all cases,
maximum security of tenure was granted. Rent, which was not
generally the prime concern of tenants, was reduced in 27.4 per cent
of cases.

TRIBUNALS IN THEORY AND PRACTICE

Chapter 3

TO FRANKS AND AFTER

'Most of the administrative tribunals with which we are familiar today are a by-product of the welfare state, and trace their authority
no further than 1911.' (1) There has, however, been a long history
to the provision of extra-judicial remedies for the grievances of
citizens against the state, or against a fellow citizen. Although
the legal system and political administration have generally been
kept separate, certain pragmatic remedies of a tribunal nature have
been available since the fourteenth century. This has occurred whenever redress could not be gained through the courts, or where a
particular area and body of knowledge required a specialised court,
or where a poor man's cause was at issue. From the Tudors onwards,
the distinguishing features of such 'courts' or appeal systems have
included the power to decide in a discretionary manner, the use of
an inquisitorial method, decision-making with reference to the demands of policy, and a swifter and more informal procedure. As such
systems themselves became too slow and cumbrous in providing
effective remedies, new bodies would arise to replace those which no
longer promised reasonable access to justice.

With the advent of the industrial revolution, means had to be
found for the implementation of the new social legislation enacted
by parliament. This need was met by a complex of national and local
boards set up to arbitrate disputes between individuals and private
companies, and later to protect the public from the economic effects,
of monopolies. In particular, the Railway and Canal Commission became a model for later tribunals by virtue of three-man membership,
its informality, the requirement to base its decisions on the concept
of 'fairness', and reference to policy rather than law.

However, it was primarily as a result of the discouraging experience of workmen's compensation under the Act of 1897, (2) that the
government of the day decided to avoid the courts by providing for
the settlement of disputes between individuals and authority by
means of a modern tribunal system such as we know today. Furthermore, in certain political circles the German system for the provision of social benefits was much admired, as was their system of
unemployment insurance and the method of settling disputes arising
therefrom, and these were copied closely in the National Insurance
Act of 1911. The local, non-legal, type of unemployment insurance

tribunal which included a workperson's representative as member, was extended to many other fields over the following twenty years. These included war pensions, the settlement of industrial disputes via Industrial Courts, the Rent Tribunal in Scotland, and widows, orphans and contributory old age pensions.

The setting up and proliferation of these administrative appeal bodies, together with the growing powers granted to Ministers in the areas of public health, welfare, slum clearance and education, began to alarm the lawyers to the extent that the Lord Chief Justice, Lord Hewart, openly attacked 'the new despotism' of the bureaucracy. As a result, the Donoughmore Committee was set up in 1931 to investigate Ministers' powers, and to look into quasi-judicial forms of decision-making. (3) This committee came to the conclusion that the fears concerning tribunals were largely groundless; however, it made reference to the need for independence where a departmental decision was at issue, and included amongst its recommendations the desirability of giving reasons for decisions, and the right of further appeal to the High Court on a point of law.

The Second World War and the social security programme of the post-war government, coming in the wake of the Beveridge Report of 1942, led to a vast expansion in the scope of the social services and the enactment of a combination of a protective and regulatory policies. The former included National Inusurance (unemployment), the National Health scheme, reorganised Industrial Injuries compensation and National Assistance. The latter included the supervision of independent schools and of voluntary homes for children, as well as the regulation of furnished rents. Tribunals were reaffirmed, or newly instituted, in order to settle disputes arising in all these areas, both between individuals and between individuals and government departments; the fact that the majority of tribunals concerned the latter was due to the great extension in the scope and administrative control of welfare resources.

After a lapse of some years, unease grew about the arbitrary powers of certain tribunals, accompanied by a growing uncertainty as to whether they were an adjunct of the administration, or part of the judicial system. Finally, the events leading to the Crichel Down Inquiry (4) acted as a catalyst for the setting up of another Committee of Enquiry, this time under the chairmanship of Lord Franks. (5) Wraith and Hutchesson, commenting on the report of this Committee, point out that 'it identifies more clearly a new phenomenon which had appeared unobtrusively on the boderline between the Administration and the Judiciary, and ... [gave] tribunals a status higher than that which they had previously enjoyed.' (6) The Committee examined the social requirements of natural justice and considered the rights of the citizen in relationship to the powers of the executive. In viewing tribunals as part of the judicial system, it was nevertheless recognised that they could not remain immune from political criticism and review, since many aspects of their administration were the direct responsibility of a particular government department, and hence directly accountable to parliament. Tribunals were described as 'the machinery provided by Parliament for adjudication rather than as part of the machinery of administration'. (7)

The Franks Report clearly accepted that tribunals had become a permanent feature of our society and in view of this, deemed it

necessary to identify their functions, constitutions and procedures and to suggest guidelines for their future operation. They
commented upon most, if not all, of the important issues pertaining
to the underlying philosophy of tribunals, as well as their operation.   In particular, they referred to the need for independence from
Ministerial control, the problem of administrative discretion, the
rights of appellants to advice and representation, the training of
personnel and the need to codify procedures. (8)   Three characteristics were identified as the hallmarks of good tribunals: openness,
fairness and impartiality, and the Committee made recommendations
designed to encourage adherence to these principles.

Foremost amongst these recommendations was the proposal to set up
a permanent supervisory body 'to keep under review the constitution
and working of the tribunals' and to ensure their independence from
those government departments whose decisions were at issue. It was
also to receive and investigate complaints from groups or individuals.
Unfortunately, although such a body, the Council on Tribunals, was
established in 1959 under the Tribunals and Enquiries Act (1958),
for the most part it has lacked the necessary power and authority to
ensure that all the recommendations of the Franks Committee were put
into effect.

In this regard, a crucial factor affecting the independence of
tribunals relates to the appointment of tribunal members. This issue
will be discussed in more detail in a subsequent chapter, but it
should be noted here that the nature of the changes made since the
Franks Committee reported has been quite minor. The Committee proposed that chairmen of tribunals, who would normally be expected to
have a legal training, should be appointed by the Lord Chancellor
and panel members by the Council on Tribunals. At the time of the
present research, chairmen were still being selected by Ministers of
the departments over whose decisions they were to adjudicate, albeit
from panels nominated by the Lord Chancellor, and they could only be
removed from office by the Lord Chancellor. (9) The appointment of
panel members also remained in the hands of the Lord Chancellor
rather than becoming the reponsibility of the Council on Tribunals.

A proposal to create a corps of tribunal clerks under the aegis of
the Lord Chancellor's office was rejected by the Committee on the
ground that it was thought not to offer a sufficiently attractive
career structure, but it was nevertheless recommended that their
duties be regulated by the Council on Tribunals. At the time of the
research, clerks were still being drawn from the ranks of the government departments involved in the dispute, although it might legitimately be argued that tribunals are now sufficiently numerous to
warrant a career structure in the form of an unattached administrative service where problems of divided loyalties would be reduced.
The implications for the independence of tribunals of this method of
appointing clerks and presenting officers will be referred to again
in the next chapter.

As one means of ensuring fairness, the Franks Committee recommended that intending applicants be made aware of their rights by the
government departments concerned, and that information should be made
available to them as to appropriate sources of advice or information.
It was also recognised that some form of legal advice scheme would
be necessary if people were to be in a position to take full advantage

of such rights, and the Committee proposed that appellants should be
entitled to representation under the Legal Aid Scheme, more
especially in those tribunals where a high degree of formality was
maintained. At the time the research was undertaken, legal aid was
not available for tribunal representation (although there was a
growing amount of free, non-legal representation) and procedures
for advising appellants varied greatly between tribunals. As we
shall later show, very few appellants are aware of their rights, or
even of where to turn for help. (10)

Openness was to be achieved, in the view of the Committee, by
making hearings open to the public whenever possible: 'We are in no
doubt that if adjudicating bodies, whether courts or tribunals, are
to inspire that confidence in the administration of justice which
is a condition of civil liberty, they should, in general, sit in
public. (11)

By the time the present study was undertaken, admission of the
public had certainly been extended, but it was by no means general
and they are excluded from the discussions surrounding the decision-
making process. Practice differed as between the three types of
tribunal studied. The Rent Tribunal usually sits in public although
it is not required to do so, and in our experience journalists,
social workers, researchers and students were generally welcomed and
there was an air of confidence amongst tribunal members about the
standards of social justice they achieved. Since the majority of
applications are by tenants, most of whom go away having had their
rent reduced or having gained some degree of security, it is, of
course, more difficult than in other types of welfare tribunal to
identify a case which is 'lost' and which may therefore be subject to
public opprobrium. (12)

National Insurance Local Tribunals are normally held in public,
but in practice few members of the public attend and they can be
asked to withdraw either by the chairmen or by the appellant. It
would appear that reference to precedent and a quite strict adherence
to the regulations set out in the relevant Acts combine to make the
tribunal members confident about the fairness of their own procedures.
Nevertheless, it is important to note that there is usually no public
access to the deliberations of the tribunal.

Supplementary Benefit Appeals are always held in private on the
grounds that appellants must be protected from public disclosure of
intimate personal and financial details. In 1971, by agreement with
the Council on Tribunals, the Supplementary Benefit (Appeal Tribunal)
Rules were amended to permit 'bona fide' research workers to be
admitted, subject to the agreement of the Chairmen and the appellants. (13) In interviews, some appellants said they felt that there
was an attempt to keep out potentially critical witnesses or representatives, a view which was no doubt reinforced by the fact that
anyone attending was asked to give evidence of his or her identity,
and to legitimate their presence. Tribunal members and officials at
Supplementary Benefit Appeals hearings appeared at times to be
somewhat defensive about the exercise of such wide-rangeing discretion, and to be uncertain about the boundaries between law and
Commission policy. In such circumstances, the privacy of the hearing
and the banning of any exact method of recording (14) may act more
as a shield for the tribunal than as a protection for the appellant.

The Franks Committee recommended that if tribunal proceedings are
to be fair to the citizen, reasons should be given for the tribunal's
decision, and there should be a right of appeal to a second or
appellate tribunal and finally to the High Court. Only rarely are
specific reasons given to the appellant and the language used often
makes it difficult for them to appreciate what is being said,
particularly when they are in an anxious state of mind. (15) Very
few of those who are dissatisfied take their case further, to the
High Court, and where such action has been taken, it is usually at
the instigation of some pressure group such as the Child Poverty
Action Group. In the case of NILTs, of course, there is the right
of appeal against a tribunal's decision to a National Insurance
Commissioner.

In addition to making recommendations, the Franks Committee
also referred to what were considered to be the advantages of
tribunals over courts: 'These ... advantages ... are cheapness,
accessibility, freedom from technicality, expedition and expert knowledge of their particular subject.' (16) Furthermore, it was argued
that the wholesale transfer to the courts of those conflicts
currently being handled by tribunals would result in the courts
being over-burdened by ever-expanding areas of dispute arising from
administrative legislation, and that the nature of such decision-
making did not normally warrant the services of scarce and expensive
judges.

The question of a comparison between the cost of tribunals and
courts did not fall within the scope of this research, and the
question of accessibility has been briefly referred to above. In
so far as expedition is concerned, we found great disparities as
between tribunals; although all those we observed tried to work to a
timetable of between three and six weeks, it was by no means certain
that appellants would not experience much greater delays. Most
expeditious were the London Rent Tribunals, a situation which can
doubtless be explained by virtue of the fact that due to the very
large number of appeals, chairmen and members worked full time.
Waiting time for these hearings did not exceed five weeks during
the period of the research, (17) and it is perhaps worth pointing
out that since most cases concerned security of tenure, some delay
may be to the advantage of the tenant, a very different situation
from that pertaining in most other types of welfare tribunal.

In the case of National Insurance and Supplementary Benefit hearings quite long delays can occur, especially away from inner London
where waiting periods of up to four months were recorded. (18) Ex-
planations given for such delays included a dearth of applications,
resulting in a decision to wait until a full half-day session could
be arranged, bureaucratic delays in investigations, administrative
errors, the difficulty of getting lay members of panels together on
the same day, and a backlog of appeals not yet dealt with. (19)
Many appellants felt that an immediate appeal to the manager of the
local office should be allowed, or that a system of appeal within
twenty-four hours to an accessible independent arbitrator should be
instituted, since even the more usual three-week delay can cause
serious hardship to a claimant whose benefit may have been with-
drawn. Any comparison with the situation pertaining to civil
disputes heard in county or magistrates' courts is of only limited

value since the immediacy of an appeal concerning income maintenance
is not paralleled in most other types of civil case. Possibly,
the issue most closely approximating an appeal for the reinstatement
of benefit would be the hearing of a case of default in maintenance
payments, and in this connection there is some evidence to suggest
that the courts may be just as expeditious as tribunals. (20)

Turning now to the question of expertise, a distinction should
be drawn between the membership of Rent Tribunals and that of the
two other types of tribunal studied. Reference was made earlier
to the discrepancy between the social background of members and
appellants and this, together with more detailed information given
in chapter 4, suggests that they do not appear to differ much from
their colleagues who sit on the bench in the magistrates' courts.
Such discrepancy results in tribunal members having little real
knowledge of the life-style of appellants, and since they are, by
and large, a much older group any experience of hardship that they
might have undergone in the past is likely to have occurred under
very different social and economic circumstances.

So far as their training and professional qualifications were
concerned, the Franks Committee's recommendation that chairmen be
legally qualified has not been generally adopted by Supplementary
Benefits Tribunals, and such persons as retired bank managers or
captains of industry, who may have had many years' experience as
ordinary panel members, may be chosen. (21) National Insurance chairmen are always legally qualified, however. Panel members at National
Insurance and Supplementary Benefits Tribunals are selected on the
one hand to represent employers or 'the Minister' and, on the other
hand, employees, or groups allied to the interests of potential
claimants. Most especially in the case of Supplementary Benefits
Tribunals, neither chairmen nor members are likely to have any
systematic knowledge of welfare law, and very few indeed have been
solely dependent on welfare benefits. A great deal of paperwork is
handed to members and they are regularly kept up to date with the
frequent amendments to the relevant Acts. However, many of them
admit that they are busy people, often with full-time careers and
almost always with heavy committments in other spheres, and so are
prevented from giving sufficient attention to the relevant literature. Specific training is not given, and it is only occasionally
that chairmen meet to review general problems of interpretation. (22)

The situation with regard to Rent Tribunals is, as was mentioned
earlier, rather different. The chairman is required to have a legal
training and to be a barrister or solicitor of not less than seven
years' standing. Such training is clearly of importance in housing
matters, since there are usually a number of important legal points;
to be clarified at the beginning of a hearing, for example as to the
validity of a notice to quit, or of a lease, the legality of a rent
book - or its very existence - and even whether the case comes within the jurisdiction of the tribunal. In very complex cases, there
may be a need to refer to the considerable amount of case law on
landlord and tenant issues. Of the panel members, one is always
an experienced valuer, and the lay person will usually be chosen for
his or her association with housing matters. He may, for example,
be an ex-housing manager of the local authority. Whilst this does
not eliminate the social discrepancy between members and applicants,

there is one further point in the Rent Tribunal procedure which helps
to reduce its significance and to increase the members' understanding
of the situation. The members of the tribunal always visit the
premises upon which they are to adjudicate, at which time they are
able to form a more realistic impression of the applicant's total
circumstances than is possible at a single meeting in the alien
environment of the tribunal hearing.

In addition to the points referred to above, Street has pointed
out that there are yet other reasons for preferring tribunals to
courts. In particular, he draws attention to the fact that politi-
cians and administrators may find the judgments given in court
wanting, in that they 'appear to disregard the social element in the
problem'. (23) He refers to a lack of confidence in the way in which
some courts interpret Acts of Parliament without examining their
underlying purpose, often preferring the inviolability of individual
property rights over the public interest.

Both Franks and Street point out that flexibility in decision-
making is largely incompatible with a system of law based on binding
precedent. They argue, in their different ways, that the growing
complexity of state schemes of benefit require a certain flexibility
of interpretation, combined with continuity and consistency of
decision-making and that this is more likely to be achieved within a
modern administrative system.

A more detailed discussion of flexibility will appear later, when
we discuss the use of discretion as it applies in our own research.
Suffice it to say here that the dichotomy between tribunals and
courts is not as clear as may at first be thought and the problems of
combining flexibility with consistency have by no means been
resolved. National Insurance Tribunals do, in fact, refer to a
system of precedent built up in the form published of Commissioner's
decisions. (24)

Supplementary Benefit Appeal Tribunals do not work on a system of
precedent, but rather use their powers of discretion within the
regulations as laid down. It is extremely difficult to achieve consistency by such a method, and a great many representatives to whom
we spoke, both legally trained and lay, commented adversely on the
arbitrary nature of the decision-making at these tribunals. Even the
chairmen and members themselves differed as to the value of their discretionary powers over wide and often complex areas of legislation,
and the lack of a higher level of appeal (other than to the High
Court on a point of law) gave even greater cause for concern on this
point.

As far as the Rent Tribunal is concerned, the area of jurisdiction
is quite limited and opportunities for using discretion are more
restricted. Policy directives from the relevant government department are quite categorical in nature (as, for example, the necessity
to comply with the Labour Government's rent freeze in the spring of
1974), and there is less uncertainty and ambiguity about policy intentions. Nevertheless, our interviews with representatives tended
to support the criticism made by Pearson concerning the inexplicable
variance in rent adjustments and periods of security awarded. (25)

The Franks Committee had suggested that the procedures adopted at
tribunal hearings should be quite formal, albeit taking place in an
informal atmosphere. 'Informality without rules of procedure may be

positively inimical to right adjudication.' (26) Despite the recommendation that representation should be available as a right, it was
hoped that the appellant would feel sufficiently at ease to be able
to talk freely, without reference to rules of evidence or other
formal court procedures, and it was thought that in such a setting,
a legal intermediary would probably prove unnecessary, thereby
avoiding what was felt to be an inappropriate adversary model.

The great majority of the chairmen and members (86 per cent)
whom we interviewed had attended a magistrates' or county court,
often in their capacity as JP, recorder, or judge, or as a legal
representative. Generally speaking, they commented favourably on
the informality of tribunals, referring to their friendliness and to
the predominance of sympathy for the appellant. They claimed that
they themselves played an advisory role as well as performing an
adjudicatory function, and the prevailing atmosphere was said to be
non-punitive. However, not all chairmen and members were so sanguine
about the situation; some pointed out that an accusatorial system
prevailed by virtue of the manner in which the presenting officers
and insurance officers pursued their duties, and that under such
circumstances an appellant can be at a severe disadvantage since so
few are legally represented. National Insurance Tribunals were
thought to be the most formal, their physical setting often resemb-
ling a courtroom. Members seemed to recognise that appellants may be
very nervous, and some thought that the very lack of formality, when
combined with an absence of information on relevant procedure,
operated to the disadvantage of appellants who were confused by the
situation.

Most of the representatives interviewed (88 per cent) had also
attended courts, though only a quarter of them had done so in their
professional capacity as lawyers. This may be explained by the fact
that whilst many had law degrees, being young they had not completed
their articles or been called to the Bar. Approximately two thirds
of the representatives referred to the greater informality and
friendliness of the tribunal setting, but as many as a third referred
to the potential for injustice arising out of a combination of the
unstructured setting and the wide use of discretion without reference
to precedent; such criticisms applied particularly to Supplementary
Benefits Tribunals. Whilst acknowledging the informality, representatives tended to think that appellants viewed courts and tribunals
in much the same light, and almost half suggested that general
nervousness was a major reason for the non-attendance of many
appellants. (27)

A little over half the appellants (56 per cent) had had experience
of courts, many as defendants or plaintiffs. Whilst the majority of
these indicated in somewhat vague and non-specific terms that their
experience in tribunals and courts was very different, they nevertheless failed to compare tribunals favourably on the basis of either
informality, the opportunity to speak freely, or the availability of
advice. Many of those attending National Insurance and Supplementary
Benefit Tribunals claimed that they were made to feel guilty in both
tribunal and court situations. By contrast, those attending Rent
Tribunals made more positive comments, mainly in respect of the re-
laxed and informal atmosphere of the tribunal.

It must be stressed, however, that a considerable number of the

appellants interviewed were quite unable to make any comparison at
all between courts and tribunals, either because they had little
objective understanding of their particular experiences, or due to
the overriding nervousness they experienced when confronted with any
kind of procedure associated with officialdom.   Their feelings of
nervousness were less related to the formality of the situation than
to their unpreparedness for conducting the appeal.   They did not know
what to expect or how to proceed.   They felt unsupported and over-
whelmed by a world of legalism and bureaucracy;   more importantly,
they simply felt frightened of the consequences of losing the case.

Informality may well be an empty goal within the present structure;
neither the chairmen and members' self-concept as 'helping' agents,
nor their attempt to deny the role identifications that appellants
associate with them, are interpreted in this way by the appellants.
To be meaningful, it seems that informality would need to be
accompanied by a widening of the composition of tribunal membership,
greater availablity of advice and representation, and the dissemina-
tion of information regarding the procedures of different welfare
tribunals.

It has taken almost a further generation of mounting criticism
and comment (28) to bring to the fore the realisation that the
problems identified by the Franks Committee still remain a very
serious handicap to the 'fair' operation of tribunals, especially
those concerned with state benefits and which affect so many people.
In theory, tribunals should be able to offer advantages over courts
in providing a forum for the protection of individual rights in the
face of expanding bureaucracy.   In practice one cannot ignore the
constraints brought to bear upon the situation by such factors as the
availability of resources, access, conflicting value systems and
inequitable power relationships.   Whilst there may not be a strong
case for making tribunals more like courts - to do so would be unlikely to solve the many problems experienced by the appellant -
certain elements of court structure and procedure might, to
advantage, be incorporated in a radical reform of tribunals. (29)
In the next three chapters, we shall discuss our research findings in
respect of three factors which we believe require urgent reconsidera-
tion: independence, discretion and representation.

Chapter 4

THE INDEPENDENCE OF TRIBUNALS

As was discussed in the preceding chapter, the independence of tribunals from Ministerial and bureaucratic control has remained a
vexed question and one causing concern at various times during the
twentieth century. It is, perhaps, the central issue: whether or
not there is a real independence from the administration or government department which may be a party to the dispute clearly affects
the degree to which impartiality can be maintained, and also the
point at which discretionary decision-making may become suspect.

'The intention of Parliament to provide for the independence of
tribunals is clear and unmistakable.' (1) This statement by the
Franks Committee went on to define independence as being: 'the
freedom of tribunals from the influence, real or apparent, of departments concerned with the subject matter of their decisions',
and in elaborating areas in which practice was falling short of intention, they referred to the importance of reviewing the method of
appointment and membership of tribunals.

CHAIRMEN AND MEMBERS: WHO ARE THEY?

In the appointment of chairmen some semblance of independence has
been achieved since the report of the Franks Committee; in the three
types of tribunals included in the research they are selected from
panels drawn up by the Lord Chancellor's office, as was suggested in
that report. However, the limited extent of their independence from
government is immediately discernible if one considers how they are
nominated to such panels in the first place.

In respect of Supplementary Benefit Appeal Tribunals, the regional
controllers of the department concerned take reponsibility for seeking out potential chairmen and conducting preliminary interviews
prior to the appointment to the Lord Chancellor's panel. Chairmen of
the Rent Tribunals are chosen by the President of the Rent Assessment
Panels. (2)

In the appointment of members the influence of the departments
concerned is even stronger since it is the managers of the local departmental offices who usually suggest names to represent 'the Minister', perhaps in consultation with the town clerk. Names may also

be suggested by currently serving chairmen. Trade unions and trades councils are invited to nominate lay members representing 'the employee', and on NILTs employers and other organisations are invited to nominate members of the other panel. As such this may be the only method of appointing members free from departmental influence or personal contacts.

Of the chairmen and members interviewed, a quarter (largely members) stated that they were selected by the local or regional office of the Department of Health and Social Security, or through a personal contact with a member of the tribunal of the Supplementary Benefits Commission. One third were selected by a union or trades council, about 4 per cent were drawn from employers' associations or the chamber of commerce, and about the same number admitted to self-nomination. Eight per cent did not know how they had come to be appointed, and most of the remainder said it was a combination of factors. Only 6 per cent were appointed directly by the Lord Chancellor's office, and this included a number of retired barristers (or those about to retire) who submitted their names with a view to serving on tribunals as legally qualified chairmen (for details see Table 4.1).

TABLE 4.1 The process by which tribunal chairmen and members were selected*

Process	%
Through trade union	33.3
Through local/regional office of DHSS/Department of Employment	16.7
Through personal contact with tribunal or DHSS	8.8
Through place of employment	7
Through Home Office or Lord Chancellor's Office	6.1
Through self-nomination	3.5
Through Chamber of Commerce or employers' association	3.5
Through the Law Society	1.8
Other (including combination of above)	11.4
Did not know	7.9
Total	100 (N=114)

* Total does not agree with sample size because one case where there is no information is excluded.

An analysis of the current social status of the chairmen and members sitting on the three tribunals studied showed that they represented only a very small section of the community: in particular ordinary wage-earners were largely excluded. (3) Apart from the restricted sources of recruitment mentioned above; a further reason for this lack of wage-earners may relate to the issue of remuneration. Whilst this is fairly generous in the case of Rent Tribunals (where we experienced most difficulty in carrying out interviews (4)), and for the chairmen of the other two types of tribunal, members receive only expenses, or time lost at work up to an amount of £5.50 per day. (5)

Seventy-three per cent of the chairmen and members interviewed came from social classes I and II; 28 per cent were retired and of the 46 per cent who were in full-time employment, most were self-employed in professional occupations, or held senior office within a trade union. (6) Reliance on the retired, self-employed and voluntary workers as tribunal members leads to a considerable social, educational, financial and age discrepancy between appellants and the decision-makers. (7) Appellants are keenly aware of this discrepancy, and in the absence of any knowledge as to who the members were at their tribunal hearing, tended to categorise them as 'middle-class', 'people who are better off', 'army officers', 'vicars' wives', 'civil servants' or 'doctors'. A very typical comment was that tribunal members are 'people who are out of touch with the hard realities of life'.

A significant factor in the overall membership is the high level of their public involvement. Over 70 per cent mentioned public service as members of other tribunals, Legal aid committees, the management committees of hospitals or educational establishments, local authority councils, trade union committees or wage councils, and 13 per cent were also serving as JPs, recorders, or judges. The picture that emerges is one of an elite holding a plurality of public positions and, as such, representing a very specific set of attitudes towards appellants.

This view of the membership was shared by many of the representatives interviewed: 25 per cent mentioned that the system of appointment interfered with the independence of the tribunal, and many more identified remoteness from working-class life as detracting from members' ability to adopt an independent stance. They also referred to the identification of tribunal members with the policies and ideologies of the 'establishment'.

A method of appointment which permits such a limited cross-section of the community to sit in judgment on issues affecting a very different part of the wider community and which, at the same time, ensures a close link between members and government departments, inevitably raises important questions of social justice.

Chairmen and members were asked whether there were any situations which they thought made their independence from departmental influence difficult to maintain. None of the Rent Tribunal membership identified such situations and 82 per cent and 75 per cent respectively, of the Supplementary Benefit and National Insurance membership answered in similar vein. It appears that most of them felt that they had genuine autonomy of action within the tribunal setting. They put forward the calibre of the membership as a basis for claiming that their independence was assured, together with lack of interference by departmental officials.

This does, however, leave a certain percentage who were not entirely convinced about their independence of action, specifically in those tribunals where departments are a party to the dispute. Some

misgivings were expressed about the presence of a clerk appointed
by the departments and from whom a chairmen may ask advice, as well
as about the bias which sometimes arises in a case as it is present-
ted by departmental officials:

'The chairmen of the tribunals hold regular meetings and are
lectured at by someone at National Level. 'X' went to the last
one and claimed, almost like the Monday club, that strikers' de-
pendants shouldn't get Social Security. The chairman doesn't
just seek the advice of the clerk, he allows him to take part in
the discussion, he's not supposed to.' (Supplementary Benefits
member.)

Sixty-nine per cent of the National Insurance and Supplementary
Benefit Tribunals chairmen and members thought they had a duty to
protect public funds and to control access to limited resources.
Some, though by no means the majority, recognised that this might be
interpreted as a means of limiting their independence:

'I know I'm sticking my neck out, in my experience, I know it's
limited, there's a tendency for the chairman and the employer's
member to support the Commissioner, because they are convinced
about protecting public funds, the chairman feels a sense of
duty.' (National Insurance Trade Union member)

Such statements make it clear that certain members are aware that independence means more than simple freedom from departmental directives.
     The particular influence of the chairman may also inhibit the
other members' freedom to contribute to the discussion and, where
there is disagreement, considerable pressure may be exerted by the
chairman in order to reach a unanimous decision. Our observations
of hearings confirmed that all tribunal chairmen tend to dominate
the proceedings, albeit in a benevolent manner when appellants are
in attendance. Of the lay members, and those representing the
'employers' or Minister, over half asked no questions and took no
part in the hearing. Of those who did take an active part, 9 per
cent took up a position interpreted by the researchers as non-
supportive of the appellant and only 8 per cent were supportive. It
seems that members rely on the chairmen because of their greater
experience (they tend to sit more often) and because of their legal
training although, as we have mentioned before, their training is
unlikely to have included a familiarity with welfare law. A more
intangible reason for such reliance seemed to derive from a feeling
that chairmen were of superior status, and members felt diffident
about pursuing points on which they differed from a 'controlling'
chairman.

DEPARTMENTAL OFFICERS: CLERKS

A major area of concern in respect of the independence of tribunals
relates to the role of the clerk. The Franks Committee was quite
definite in suggesting that the 'duties of the clerk should be

confined to secretarial work ... like a magistrates' clerk he should be debarred from retiring with the tribunal when they consider their decision.' (8) According to our observations of the three tribunals, in 87 per cent of hearings, clerks were allowed to remain in the room with the tribunal members when the decision was considered. The following comments refer to the overall role of the clerk at all the observed hearings, but as the researchers were allowed to be present during the deliberations in only 44 per cent of such hearings (in the case of National Insurance Tribunals this was allowed in only 14 per cent of the cases), our comments on the role of the clerk during the deliberations refer only to this smaller number.

In the main, both during the hearing and the deliberations, the clerk restricted his role to that of basic administration: taking notes, reading out letters, answering factual queries and so forth. Some would give information to the appellant, or to the tribunal, concerning the relevant Act or regulations relating to the case. National Insurance clerks appeared the least likely to extend their role beyond that of basic administration.

In Rent Tribunals, the procedure is somewhat different since all hearings are open to the public and usually all the applicants, their witnesses and representatives, will be present together awaiting the hearing. Tribunal members would either retire from the room, go behind a screen or huddle together and deliberate in low voices within the same room. In only 3 per cent of observed cases did the clerks take a particularly active role beyond that of giving information, and in only 5 per cent of hearings did they retire with the tribunal members.

The problem of involvement relates essentially to Supplementary Benefit Tribunal clerks: in 15 per cent of observed cases they took an active role in the hearing and in a further 11 per cent of cases they were involved in the subsequent deliberations and had the opportunity to influence decisions. It must be stressed that this latter figure relates only to those deliberations witnessed by researchers, and the overall influence may be far more pervasive than we are aware of. As Herman pointed out, 'clerks frequently interpret Commission policies to tribunal members', (9) and indeed tribunal members often turn to the clerk to seek information and guidance about the law and permissible discretion. Clerks are supposed to be barred from such involvement by departmental instruction, but in our experience, such functions are still carried out by them, (10) even to the extent of initiating suggestions for a decision. (11)

It would seem that the degree to which the clerk is involved in influencing the tribunal decision is dependent upon several factors: the complexity and breadth of coverage of the relevant law, the extent to which decisions are based upon precedent or are amenable to discretionary judgments, the expertise of the tribunal membership, and the identification of the clerk with the government department whose decisions are the subject of appeal. On all these counts, it is hardly surprising that the Supplementary Benefit Appeal Tribunal clerk more often takes an active role than clerks to other tribunals, on a continuum which can vary between advice and domination. There would appear to be a strong case for reviewing the idea of a central corps of clerks to service all tribunals, a proposal which

was earlier rejected by the Franks Committee. The main objective
of such an arrangement would be the clear impartiality of the clerk.
(12) It must nevertheless be recognised that a change of this
nature, to be effective, might need to be accompanied by a scheme
of training for tribunal members in order that they might carry out
their duties without leaning unduly on the clerks for advice and
information.

DEPARTMENTAL OFFICERS: PRESENTING AND INSURANCE OFFICERS

Herman, in his analysis of the role and consequent behaviour of presenting officers at Supplementary Benefit Tribunal hearings,
comments:

> An independent appeal process may be jeopardised by the ex-
> ceptionally eager presenting officer whose responsibilities have
> been increased by the recent changes in the relative responsibi-
> lities of clerks and presenting officers. (13)

He was referring to the fact that members of the departmental
staff had been specifically designated as full-time presenting
officers and that, as such, they were more likely to feel under
pressure to produce a satisfactory record of appeals 'won' (i.e.
disallowed) than had been the case when tribunal work had been
merely one aspect of a local manager's total workload. Herman argues
that in a situation where their career prospects may be dependent
upon their performance in this very specialised area, such officers
might face a dilemma when required to give information which might
ultimately weaken their own case. New instructions from DHSS had
required that questions of law be referred to the presenting
officer rather than to the clerk because of the recognised
ambiguity of the clerk's role in the hearing. (14) However, since
both are employees of the relevant department, it would seem to be an
inappropriate solution to transfer the ambiguous role from one
officer to another. In practice, Supplementary Benefit Appeal
clerks still tend to perform the role which has, in theory, been
re-allocated to the presenting officer.
   The full-time insurance officer at National Insurance Local Tribunals is in much the same position, and his specialised function,
whilst seemingly a rationalisation of the procedures, in practice
places a similar onus on him to 'win' cases – that is cases which
are upheld by Commissioner's decisions. (15) Theoretically, neither
the presenting officer nor the insurance officer are supposed to act
as 'advocates' for their respective departments, rather they are
there to 'assist' at the hearing. Our own observations suggest a
discrepancy between what is supposed to be their role and what is
their role, and that not only do they act as advocates for their departments, but that on occasion their behaviour could be interpreted as openly antagonistic towards the appellant. This 'antagonism', which in the view of the research workers occurred at 21
per cent of the National Insurance hearings and 24 per cent of the
Supplementary Benefit hearings, consisted of making derogatory re-
marks or comments about an appellant, especially if he or she were

absent. (16) Other manifestations of such an attitude included in-
terrogating an appellant, often on personal issues at some remove
from the question in dispute, (17) or very vociferously making the
case against a nervous, inarticulate, and usually unrepresented
claimant. (18)

Members and officials were for the most part on friendly terms as
they would meet together frequently at hearings and tended to confirm each other in lines of reasoning, especially where the decision
had gone against the appellant. One National Insurance Tribunal
appellant complained bitterly that due to the lack of separate waiting facilities, he was unwittingly drawn into an intimate conversation with someone who turned out to be the insurance officer. Such
conversations were also observed by the researchers taking place
before the Supplementary Benefit Tribunal hearings where anxious
and confused appellants might be casting around for information, un-
aware that the person from whom they sought it would soon be
arguing against their case in the tribunal hearing. In these
circumstances some officers fail to declare themselves as interested
parties and such practices reflect poorly upon any general standards
of impartiality or justice.

The situation at Rent Tribunals is, of course, very different because the adjudication concerns disputes between private individuals
and there is no government department involved in the case. At the
hearings observed, only 17 per cent of the professional advocates
appearing on behalf of the landlords relied very heavily on cross-
examination of the tenant; in other words, they were less likely
than were departmental officials to pursue aggressive tactics towards the applicant and, where this did happen, they were quite
firmly controlled by the chairman.

The view that clerks and presenting officers introduce bias into
the proceedings was shared by the representatives interviewed.
Many commented on the reliance of panel members on departmental
officers, due to their own lack of expertise and to the emphasis
which such officers place upon their interpretation of Commission
policy.

Appellants were not asked directly whether they thought that tribunals were independent bodies, but in the course of interviews many
of them commented on the bias of the tribunal members towards the
views of departmental officers, and their seeming unwillingness to
use discretion if it appeared to conflict in any way with members'
views, unrepresentativeness and their lack of relevant expertise.
All these factors combined together to bring into question the
'fairness' or impartiality of the proceedings, and to render their
independence suspect.

Chapter 5

THE USE OF DISCRETION

In matters of administrative disputes, one important reason for preferring a tribunal to a system of adjudication through the courts
was said to be the desire for flexibility in the interpretation of
relevant Acts of Parliament as applied to individual cases. As has
been pointed out by Street, statutes 'use words like "fair",
"adequate" and "reasonable", intending that these standards shall be
applied to particular cases in the light of experience'. (1) For
this reason, decision-making in tribunals is subject to the application of a considerable degree of discretion which varies between
different types of tribunal. In so far as welfare benefits are
concerned the extent of the discretionary powers available to the
tribunal reflects in large measure the degree to which such powers
are available to administrators at a prior stage in the normal
distribution of welfare resources.

NATIONAL INSURANCE LOCAL APPEALS

It is generally mooted that the amount of discretion available to
the National Insurance Local Appeal Tribunal is much less than that
available to the Supplementary Benefits Appeal Tribunal, because
appeals are supposed to be decided by reference to a clear body of
case law with which the legally qualified chairman is deemed to be
familiar. It is also said that 'they are much more likely to
adjourn cases where they have not got sufficient evidence to form
a decision'. (2) Whilst our own observations certainly confirm
this latter point (14 per cent of National Insurance cases are
adjourned as compared with only 5 per cent of Supplementary Benefit
cases), we are by no means certain that the element of discretion
in decision-making is as limited as would at first appear. Indeed,
as another commentator has pointed out, 'there are wide areas of
discretion within the national insurance framework. The more
obvious cases like industrial misconduct or just cause for leaving
employment turn on disputed facts where the tribunal has to weigh
each party's story.' (3)
   Often, there seems to be very little to choose between the argument advanced by one appellant as compared with another, yet the

decision of the tribunal may be quite different. For example, in respect of a late claim for sickness benefit, a young man made the mistake of sending his certificate to his employer and it was not forwarded to the Department of Health and Social Security until too late. He lost his claim to benefit and was told to try and get his trade union representative at work to persuade the employers to pay, since they could be deemed to have been negligent. Then followed the case of a young woman who claimed out of time and did not appear before the tribunal, but who had her claim accepted in the light of the Insurance Officer's amended submission that she was mentally confused and incapable of conducting her own affairs. The chairman commented that she was not the normal type of 'scrounger' but some-one who was genuinely inadequate. Decisions are often affected by such unsubstantiated notions of who is 'deserving' or 'undeserving', and who should or should not be expected to 'stand on their own feet'. Nevertheless, the National Insurance Tribunals' sympathy for or antipathy towards the appellant is not allowed to interfere with statutory provisions, to the extent that it may do at a Supplemen-tary Benefit hearing. (4)

However, similar discretional attitudes are displayed by panels at both types of tribunal and the previous work record of a claimant is as likely to have as much attention paid to it as the immediate circumstances surrounding a decision to leave employment. (5) From our observations at National Insurance Local Tribunals, it would seem that value judgments are almost universally expressed about cases although the potentially adverse effect of such judgments may be thwarted by the inability to pinpoint an adequate reason for refusing to reverse an appealed decision. For instance, in a case of alleged misconduct where a man refused to work longer hours than the agreed minimum, members of the panel indulged their prejudice (in his absence) by calling the appellant a 'hothead', a 'thorough nuisance of a man', 'he sounds an absolute shocker', but they were unable to find against him due to the fact that there was no evi-dence that actual performance fell below acceptable atandards.

SUPPLEMENTARY BENEFIT APPEALS

It is in the area of Supplementary Benefits that most misgivings arise in relation to the degree of discretion and the manner in which it is exercised. In this area, the notion of rights or eligibility is not backed by an insurance principle, i.e., paid contributions to which benefits are clearly linked, nor by any simi-lar structure of rights and obligations, i.e., a tenant paying rent for accommodation for which he will expect a certain standard of provision and potential security. Although in the areas of National Insurance benefit, or the right to accommodation, the ultimate power may lie with the adminstrator or the landlord, there is never-theless in the mind of the claimant or tenant, the notion of a right that has been paid for.

For most supplementary benefit claimants, excepting the militant few, (6) this is not the case, and benefit is regarded as 'charity'. So long as they perceive the prevailing morality as insisting that benefit must be 'earned' either through work or the payment of a

contribution, they do not conceptualise it as a 'right'. Some
claimants may be able to point to a lifetime of taxes paid with
never a penny claimed, but many more cannot, and the system is designed to maintain a minimum income for people temporarily, or
sometimes permanently, without sufficient alternative resources,
irrespective of any kind of financial contribution. In this sense,
the system itself is totally discretionary, except in terms of the
specified rates of benefit, for it is the administration which
decides whether to award benefit in the first instance, and when
and on what grounds to curtail or remove it. (7) There is considerable evidence that conditions for removing benefit, such as the
four-week rule, the wage-stop and the cohabitation rule are
applied in an arbitrary and contradictory manner, and the policy
guidelines and internal documents of the Commission are often in-
consistently followed. (8)

The many and varied levels of potential discretion have, on
occasion, brought the supplementary benefits system into considerable disrepute. Bull points out that the principle behind the inequitable and discretionary treatment of claimants bears little
relation to their particular needs and resources. In reaching a
decision reference tends to be made to the poorest section of the
larger community which is not dependent on benefits. It is considered inequitable to award a basic benefit or exceptional needs
payment beyond the reach of many people in full-time work, on the
assumption that the work ethic would be so undermined by a systema-
tised, clear and adequate method of income maintenance, that a large
number of people would prefer to sit back happily and be supported
by 'welfare'. Such a philosophy ignores the fact that the majority
of claimants are the old, the sick and disabled, and women with
dependent children. In 1973, only 9 per cent of recipients of
supplementary benefits were officially defined as unemployed (9)
and this group is constantly pressurised by the Commission to re-
enter the employment market. Claimants thus defined are periodi-
cally interviewed by Unemployment Review Officers whose 'aim is to
find out why a claimant cannot get or keep a job and, if possible,
to help him deal with any difficulties which prevent him from doing
so'. (10) Benefit may even be made conditional on attendance at a
Reestablishment Centre, 'their function being to help men who have
been unemployed for a long time to overcome the deleterious effect
of this, and to re-acquire the habit of working'. (11) Discretion
is the cornerstone of a system where primary eligibility may be
removed almost at the whim of departmental officers, for example on
suspicion of sexual relations under the cohabitation rule, a be-
havioural measure that may have no connection with financial
circumstances. The Supplementary Benefits Appeal Tribunals reflect
this preoccupation with moral worth and the work ethic, combined with
sympathy for those cases which can easily be defined as 'deserving'.
The following cases drawn from our research data have been selected
in order to illustrate the mixture of attitudes which may result in
either unrestricted largesse or a stony refusal.

Case 1

Mrs X, a deserted wife with three children, applied to the Commission for an exceptional needs payment to cover removal expenses to another city. The lowest quotation she had obtained was for an amount around £100. The Commission refused to pay. At the appeal, the woman pointed out that she would be returning to her home town and family, that her mother would be able to look after the children and that if her depression and isolation could be so alleviated, then she would be able to return to her skilled occupation. In considering the case, the decision to award the money was based upon the argument that the Commission by an astute payment now, might be able to avoid long-term support of the family if the mother could be enabled to return to work.

Case 2

Miss B, an old lady of 82, made a similar appeal against the refusal of the Commission to pay her removal expenses of £16.50 when she was rehoused. She was refused because she was reported to have capital assets in excess of £160. The old lady was unable to attend and explain her reasons for requesting assistance. Although the Minister's member commented that the cost of funerals was very high today and that the old lady might be saving her money for this purpose, it was finally decided not to finance the removal expenses. The argument put forward was that the State should not be made responsible, since it could not expect to receive any money left over after her death, despite helping to support her now. (In theory the Commission may ignore quite a large amount of capital savings, but in practice many claimants are forced to part with precious savings and assets, with progressively less chance of replacing them.)

Case 3

A young man, Mr Y, appealed against a decision to reduce his benefit by 40 per cent made on the grounds that he had 'no just cause' for giving up his employment. Mr Y explained that he had expected to be offered a full-time job with a Housing Association with which he had worked as a volunteer, and he brought supportive evidence to this effect. Unfortunately, the job fell through, but by this time the prevous job had already been given up and he applied for benefit. At the time of the appeal, he had already found work. The appeal was lost, the chairman explaining that because the first job was not what the young man wanted, that did not make it necessarily 'unsuitable' and that he had no right to give up employment on the mere chance of a preferred occupation. (The implication is that the Commission has the right to 'penalise' anyone giving up work, despite evidence to show that a particular person was only temporarily dependent and not habitually 'work shy'.)

In all three cases, we are paraphrasing the actual argument behind the decisions made. Despite the fact that in 1971 directives
were given to the effect that full reasons for decisions were to
be disclosed as a matter of course, (12) this is rarely done and
the information given to the appellant and recorded on the office
files does not in any way reflect the reality of the deliberations,
even where a decision goes in the appellant's favour.

In such a highly discretionary system, the lack of precedent
creates particular problems, not least for representation since,
no previous decision may be quoted in support of a case, (13) On
the other hand tribunal members may refuse to go beyond Commission
policy guidelines on the grounds of a need for consistency. Our
own observations confirm that presenting officers 'tend to quote
Commission policy as though it were legally binding on the tribunal .... It is not uncommon for them to suggest, for instance,
that a decision favourable to the claimant will result in a flood of
similar appeals and a massive drain on public funds. (14)

RENT TRIBUNAL APPEALS

The situation with regard to the discretion exercised by the Rent
Tribunal is very different from that in the other two types of
tribunal. In essence only two matters are covered by appeals in
respect of furnished tenancies: the determination of rent and
security of tenure. Occasionally, the prior question of jurisdiction has to be decided, for example whether a tenancy falls outside
the tribunal's jurisdiction either because it could be described as
unfurnished, or a fixed-term tenancy, or where it is claimed that
board is provided. Such questions would, however, be decided by
reference to legal precedent and even though this might allow some
leeway, there could still be a consensus between members of the
tribunal, representatives and appellants as to the factors relevant
to the decision-making process. (15)

Since members of Rent Tribunals often sit also on Rent Assessment Panels (concerned with determining rents for unfurnished
premises), the method of fixing a 'reasonable' rent in the case of
furnished accommodation appeared to approximate quite closely the
criteria set out in part IV of the Rent Act for the determination
of a 'fair' rent, that is, having regard 'to the age, character and
locality of the dwelling-house and to its state of repair',
irrespective of scarcity value. (16) The presence of an experienced valuer in both instances provided some consistency with
reference to determining the value of the premises and at all the
hearings attended the chairman would begin by describing in detail
the extent, state of repair, and provision of furniture and
services at the premises in question. With the advent of the 1974
Rent Act covering both furnished and unfurnished premises, the
common application of these criteria has been officially established.

Discretion with regard to security could only operate within the
six-month period specified in the legislation. However, within this
comparatively regulated situation, there was often criticism relating to the way in which discretion was exercised, (17) and at a
wider level, attention was frequently drawn to the inadequacy of

current legislation and the appeals procedure, as a means of solving
the long-term problem of security for furnished tenants.

Whilst the Rent Tribunal compares favourably with the other types
of tribunal studied, in respect of experienced membership, procedure and, especially, awareness of the larger social problems involved where housing is concerned, it was nevertheless noted that
the tribunal's powers were generally being used in a somewhat conservative way, especially where an important point of law might be
involved.

Case 1

Miss D was said to be a weekly 'boarder' in a bed and breakfast
establishment on the south coast. However, she contended that she
was really a furnished tenant as she did not receive a·cooked breakfast but was given a few basic provisions on a tray which she then
prepared herself in her own room. She claimed that the amount of
food received did not actually amount to 'board'. The landlady had
evicted her from the establishment and Miss D was asking the Rent
Tribunal to accept that the case fell within their jurisdiction
and to grant her some security. The landlady had engaged a London
barrister and the 'boarder' had engaged a solicitor. The two legal
representatives and the Chairman spent two hours referring to
earlier cases and consulting law books regarding the definition of
'substantial' part of the rent and 'board'. Both parties were also
cross-examined by the opposing sides. Eventually, it was decided
that the case did not fall within their jurisdiction, a decision
which was accepted with evident relief by the panel members since it
enabled them to avoid setting a new precedent in respect of the
weekly boarder category - though this generalised possiblity was
never referred to. (18)

Case 2

Mrs H applied for an extension of security in respect of her
furnished basement flat. Her husband was unable to attend the hearing because he was working. The couple had a child aged three.
There had been a fire in the flat a few months before, and the
'welfare' had offered them one room and a kitchen at the top of an
old house but this they refused because of the wife's asthma. The
landlord refused to pay for redecorating the flat and would make no
claim on his insurance. Consequently, the couple did all the
necessary redecorating and rewiring but had withheld an amount of
rent in lieu of this. The landlord did not attend the hearing in
person and his solicitor made much of the admitted arrears. The
landlord's professed reason for requiring possession was to enable
him to sell the house but the tenant pointed out that this was not
feasible (at least not with vacant possession), since the upstairs
flat was let unfurnished and the tenants had no intention of moving
out. The couple had been on the council waiting list for three
years but as yet had been offered nothing. They could not find any
other privately rented place at a price they could afford. If

evicted, the family would become homeless and would probably be
split up. Despite commenting on this disastrous possibility and
stating that the only possible loss to the landlord would be financial (not being able to realise his capital), the Chairman finally
announced that only two months security would be awarded 'for the
sake of the child', and that the arrears must be paid immediately.
This money had already been put aside and offered by the couple as
soon as responsibility over the fire could be worked out. The wife
(unrepresented) was quite shocked and left the hearing very upset.

This second case is more 'typical' in that it does not involve
any unusual points of law, but rather the way in which 'discretion'
is exercised. One could not even say that the case was 'lost' since
some security was given, but this finding, even if it had been for
the maximum period, was completely inadequate in relation to the
need for security of this family. (19) It is not intended here to
criticise in any one-sided fashion the operation of the Rent
Tribunal. There were many instances observed where maximum security
was given or where the tribunal members effected some conciliation
between landlord and tenant, or between antagonistic tenants and, as
was mentioned earlier, an entirely 'lost' case is rare. In certain
situations minimum security was actually agreed upon by tribunal and
applicant jointly, for example in an effort to bring pressure upon
the Local Authority to take responsibility for rehousing the tenant.
But there were also examples where even the discretionary powers
available were insufficient to deal with the overwhelming issue of
long-term security which was arbitrarily based upon whether premises
were furnished or not, a situation now changed by the 1974 Act.

PROBLEMS IN THE USE OF DISCRETION

So far as tribunal members were concerned, it is perhaps paradoxical
that the Supplementary Benefits panel were least satisfied with the
amount of discretion available to them, almost half of them claiming
that their discretionary powers were too limited and needed to be
widened. This obtains despite the fact that of the three types
studied, this tribunal has the most opportunity to use discretion,
the system itself being to a large extent a discretionary one at all
levels. Their particular dissatisfaction would seem to require
some explanation.
Supplementary Benefit Tribunal members seem to feel that there
are more cases which are 'deserving' than the tribunal is able to
help. Allied to this is the fact that the legislation is complex,
and frequently being amended, and members often rely on Commission
policy as expounded by its officers rather than looking for possi-
bilities which lie outside such policy, yet within the law. Some
feel that scale rates are too low but they can find no grounds on
which to improve a claimant's regular income and in any case they
fear that an extensive use of discretionary powers would cause in-
equity vis-à-vis other claimants. Furthermore, although their
powers range across a wide spectrum, they are often interpreted as
being limited to particular instances, for example, additional
dietary allowances are usually restricted to persons suffering from
rather specific medical complaints.

It is possible that the absence of general guidelines or clear
definitions by which to judge cases confuses the panels and makes
them feel the need for more discretion in order to deal with cases
that do not fit into any easily identifiable category. Such an
analysis might offer some explanation as to why panels find it so
difficult to make judgments in borderline cases, for instance,
whether a spastic child qualifies for an additional dietary allowance, or whether squatters living in the same premises may be considered as separate householders. Such adjudications are experienced
as much more problematic than deciding whether or not a claimant may
be given money for a pair of shoes or to settle an unpaid electricity
bill. Cases concerning right to benefit after refusal or disqualification are even more complex and challenging to the 'controlling
versus benevolence' conflict which underlies the system as a whole.

Herman claims that the tribunal finds most difficulty in the
identification of relevant 'exceptional circumstances', (20) but
our observations and interviewing indicate that this area of freedom
under the legislation is actually more successfully coped with by
reference to the economic, ethical and moral constructs which the
tribunal members bring to the cases. Whether these meet the intentions of policy or not is another question. Free-reined judgment
does not present too many difficulties to tribunal members, though
it may to the unprepared and disappointed appellant, but disputed
areas of adequacy, categorisation and eligibility do, and the intervention of the traditional legalistic representative is probably
most relevant in such cases; non-legal representatives are
probably more useful in supporting the appellant and providing evidence relevant to an 'exceptional needs' appeal.

Herman has also pointed out that the Supplementary Benefit
Tribunals exercise discretion in ways other than the actual decision-making, for instance over procedural issues like the sharing of
documents (21) and that they differ in the thoroughness of their
enquiries into assertions of fact, particularly with regard to the
Commission's submission. (22) Our observations indicated that
Supplementary Benefits panels are quick to 'sum-up' appellants and
to stereotype them: 'malingerer', 'immoral', or 'undeserving' are
terms which are all too readily attached to individuals, and 'un-
married mothers', 'students' or 'strikers' are examples of group
stereotypes, all bearing a pejorative connotation. Furthermore, if
an appellant or his representative fails to appear at the hearing
there tends to be an automatic and quite explicit assumption that
the appeal must be a frivolous or unjustified one, even, at times, in
the face of written submissions and genuine reasons for non-attendance.

The fact that a high degree of discretionary power is synonomous
with power over access to resources (i.e., benefit) results in many
claimants being forced to recognise their powerlessness and to con-
form to stereotypes which deny both their own integrity and the
'reality' of their situation. Even then, the 'rules of the game'
may have their pitfalls; a family that cannot cope may be treated
unsympathetically just because they are seen as not making enough
effort, and another family may forfeit sympathy because they are
trying hard to maintain respectability and coping reasonably well.

There has already been considerable criticism and agitation for the introduction of curbs on the discretionary powers of Supplementary Benefit Tribunals, either in terms of a completely 'legalised' system (23) or by injecting stricter rules of procedure, improved representation and instituting a further level of appeal. Certainly, representatives at Supplementary Benefit hearings were worried about the amount of discretion available to the tribunal. One such representative commented: 'They understand the Act imperfectly, and often make unconstitutional decisions. On occasion they use discretion against the law without knowing it.' A great many mentioned that the powers of panel members were used too discriminatingly, appellants being categorised as 'deserving', or 'undeserving' a criticism much less frequently heard from National Insurance appeals representatives and not at all by Rent Tribunal representatives.

In the case of National Insurance Tribunals the opposite was sometimes the case, namely they were criticised for being too flexible. There are those who argue that where there is an insurance basis to a claim for benefit, disqualifications like those which involve time limits are unjust and need to be repealed so that they are no longer the concern of the tribunal. Where there is a discretionary element present, the importance of appellants' having an experienced representative to counteract the arguments of the Insurance Officer and improve the 'balance' of the proceedings is at its most obvious.

Commentators such as Richard Titmuss (24) and Kenneth Culp Davis (25) have pointed out that many areas of discretion exist even within a judicial system which is generally considered to be subject to a strict set of rules. The argument then revolves around whether it is preferable to find ways whereby the amount of discretion should be circumscribed by the introduction of more legal rules into administrative adjudication, or whether individualised justice is better served by maintaining and maximising the amount of discretion currently available.

Fulbrook et al. refer to the need for a 'greater degree of orderliness which will lead to greater justice for the individual applicant'. Our own observations and the responses to interviews concerning Supplementary Benefits Appeals would seem to support their argument for a more judicial approach. (26)

Chapter 6

THE ROLE OF REPRESENTATION

Whatever changes and improvements are brought about in the structure, membership and procedure of tribunals, certain areas of dispute will inevitably remain, particularly in relation to access to welfare benefits controlled by government depatments. It is generally mooted, (1) that the best way of protecting the appellant's interests within a structure which is frequently imperfect, and often highly discretionary, is to ensure access to advice and skilled representation. However, there is considerable disagreement about the best sources of such help and how it should be financed. (2)

It would, furthermore, be unwise to consider representation as a panacea which will remove all the problems encountered by persons appealing to tribunals, and it is necessary to explore quite specifically at which type of tribunal, and for what kind of case, representation is suitable or desirable. Furthermore, there is a need to consider what kind of representative provides the most advantageous service (from the client's point of view) and under what circumstances, as well as what kind of support services are needed to 'back up' representation.

REPRESENTATIVES: INTERVIEWS AND OBSERVATIONS

Reference was made earlier (see chapter 2, p. 12) to the background characteristics of the 103 representatives interviewed. The largest group (25 per cent) were trade union officials, followed by social workers and solicitors, the remainder being drawn from various voluntary agencies and different types of advice centres. (3) Two-thirds were not legally trained, and of those who had such training, the majority were solicitors. Half the representatives had had experience of more than one type of tribunal, though most had represented fewer than six appellants during the preceding twelve months. Sixty per cent of the representatives had been involved in such work for under three years, probably a reflection of the age distribution of the sample, but nearly a quarter had been involved in similar activities for over ten years.

Most thought that tribunal representation should form part of the normal job of a solicitor or social worker. About a quarter said that their involvement came out of participation in the trade union movement, and since many of these were paid officials of the larger unions, representing members at tribunals was part of their job. Twenty-eight per cent came to represent appellants at tribunals as a result of voluntary work undertaken in the community and only a small proportion said that their representational work grew out of personal experience as a claimant, or as a member of one of the newer self-help groups (Table 6.1).

TABLE 6.1   How representatives became involved with tribunals

	%
Through job (social worker, solicitor, etc.)	36.9
Through trade union movement	23.3
Through voluntary work	28.2
Through personal experience as claimant or tenant	7.8
Other	3.8
Total	100 (N=100)

Like chairmen and members, representatives tended to be highly involved in local groups and activities, but their participation took the form of pressure group membership rather than sitting on official bodies and management committees. A quarter belonged to a trade union and a fifth to a political party; a significant number also belonged to organisations or groups offering some type of social service.

As might be expected, representatives held very positive views about the value of representation in terms of the advantages obtained by a clear presentation of cases, and the use of advocacy skills on behalf of individual appellants. Despite the fact that only about half of them felt that their intervention would give the appellant a better chance of 'success', they were nevertheless very much in favour of the £25 advice scheme and of the extension of legal aid to cover representation. Many specifically mentioned that this should be extended on a fee for service basis to non-legal representatives or agencies.

Any discussion of the performance of the representatives in action must be interpreted with caution since although in 48 of the 276 observed appeals the case was presented by someone other than the appellant, most of these were friends or relatives. Amongst what might be termed 'official' representatives (and therefore falling within the definition for research purposes), most were trade unionists or members of the Claimants' Union and only very few were solicitors.

Most of those observed at hearings structured their case around the individual needs of the appellant and stressed the special nature of their client's case. However, some preferred to rely on a systematic presentation of the facts, which they believed spoke for themselves, a technique which proved most effective in Supplementary Benefit Tribunals.

Where lawyers appeared, they often seemed either ill-prepared or insufficiently acquainted with the relevant areas of law; unfortunately, when this was not the case they sometimes tended to antagonise the tribunal members by their intense legalism, again a situation which was most often resisted by members of Supplementary Benefit Tribunals.

As might be expected, lack of familiarity with the relevant legislation was even more apparent amongst non-lawyers, although they often had a much better general understanding of the nature of the case and its background than did the lawyer, as well as being more accustomed to tribunal procedure.

It was clear that the majority of appellants were unable to present their own case with any confidence, though they could express themselves in a roundabout and inarticulate fashion. The support offered by the presence of a representative seemed to reduce their anxiety and encouraged them to take part in the proceedings in a more meaningful way.

Observation of the role played by the representative suggests that he or she is able to modify some of the negative features of the tribunal system to which reference was made earlier - lack of independence, the unrepresentative nature of the tribunal membership, the dominating role of the chairman and the dependence on departmental officers. A skilled representative can redress the imbalance caused by such situations, more especially where the conflict is one between the individual appellant and a government department.

ATTENDANCE

We have already given statistics showing the relationship between attendance and representation (see Chapter 2, p.28), and clearly these two factors are both related to successful outcome: a represented case is more likely to be attended, and attendance usually disposes the tribunal to give the case more serious consideration. (4) Attended cases are awarded more time both for hearing and deliberation than are unattended ones (see Table 6.2) and the longer period spent on Rent Tribunal cases no doubt reflects the high attendance rate at that type of tribunal (see Table 6.3).

TABLE 6.2 Observed length of case according to type of tribunal*

Length	NILTs % cases	SBATs % cases	RTs % cases
Less than $\frac{1}{4}$ hour	53.5	41.4	27.9
$\frac{1}{4}$ hour - less than $\frac{1}{2}$ hour	28.7	36.9	42.6
$\frac{1}{2}$ hour or longer	17.8	20.7	29.5
Total	100 (N=101)	100 (N=111)	100 (N=61)

* Totals may not agree with sample size as cases where there is no information are excluded.

TABLE 6.3 Observed attendance and representation according to type of tribunal

	NILTs cases	SBATs cases	Rts cases
Attendance	42.6%	54.8%	85.5%
Representation	17.9%	18.5%	14.5%
Total	(N=101)	(N=113)	(N=62)

Not only do the data indicate the importance of attendance at all three tribunals, it was also one of the issues about which chairmen and members felt most strongly. As many as half of them thought that non-attendance by appellants created problems, though this was less frequently mentioned by Rent Tribunal chairmen and members. Fifty-three per cent of all those interviewed made reference to work committments as constituting a valid reason for non-attendance, and yet only one or two members suggested that an evening hearing would offer some solution to this problem. Thirty-one per cent of members thought that non-attendance indicated a frivolous appeal and from our observations we can confirm that many unattended cases were treated as so much dross at the end of a hearing.

TABLE 6.4 Reasons for non-attendance by appellants at tribunal hearings as posited by chairmen and members* **

Reason	% of chairmen and members stating these views
Work	52.6
Frivolous appeal`	30.8
Sickness; poor health	30.7
Appellant sees no chance of success	24.6
Apathy; resignation	18.5
Nervousness	17.5
Distance; transport difficulties	13.1
Appellant satisfied with explanation on appeal documents	11.4
Appellant is elderly	8.8
Family responsibilities	2.6
Other or additional reasons given	21.1

*   Totals exceed 100 per cent (N=114) since many interviewees gave more than one reason.
** Total does not agree with sample size because one case where there is no information is excluded.

About a quarter of the chairmen and members interviewed thought that appellants who did not attend avoided doing so because they felt they did not stand any chance of success (see Table 6.4).

Our interviews with those appellants who did not attend confirmed that as many as 22 per cent did indeed think they had little chance of success, but this was not necessarily the main reason for their non-attendance, it was simply a contributory factor. Furthermore, for them the feeling that they would not be successful was in no way related to the frivolity of the appeal, rather it was due to the perceived impossibility of 'winning' against a government bureau-cracy. Herman has pointed out that some frustrated appellants at Supplementary Benefit Appeal Tribunals appeal against the pitiful scale rates that the tribunal is powerless to adjust. (5) Whilst some chairmen and members may consider such appeals as 'frivolous' they are certainly not seen in this light by the appellants, who often have very little understanding of the limits of the tribunals' jurisdiction. The majority gave specific and seemingly valid reasons for their non-attendance.· Either they were working - perhaps in a new job where they did not like to ask for time off - or they were ill, or suffered from some long-term disability which made travel difficult. Some had family commitments and could not find a child minder, others had no money to pay the fares, often a consider-able item when travelling from outlying districts, and they were not sure that they would be reimbursed. (6) One man mentioned that he had no decent clothes to wear and felt ashamed to appear. Quite a few mentioned the lack of a representative or someone to speak in an articulate fashion on his or her behalf: 'I thought it would be no good without a representative. I can't put my case and feelings into words.'

TABLE 6.5   Reasons given by interviewed appellants and applicants for their non-attendance at the tribunal hearing*

Reason	% of appellants who did not attend
Work	27.4
Sickness; poor health	27.3
Appellant saw no chance of success	22.9
Nervousness	13.6
No confidence in the tribuanl	9.1
Did not realise the significance of attendance	7.0
Distance; transport difficulties	4.6
Family responsibilities	2.3
On holiday	2.3
Other or additional reasons given	27.9

* Totals add to more than 100 per cent (N=44) since many respondents
  gave more than one reason.

Our interviews suggested that in many instances their cases were
extremely complex and the persons concerned were often those least
well equipped to deal with the situation. (7) Age, nerves, and
disabilities of various kinds made it impossible for them either
to attend or to have the capacity to find a suitable representative. (8)

Representatives interviewed had a much more accurate and detailed knowledge than did chairmen and members of why some appellants did not attend hearings, in particular, 44 per cent (as
compared with 18 per cent of chairmen and members) thought that
appellants felt very nervous, a situation likely to inhibit attendance, and far fewer considered the appeal to be frivolous - 12 per
cent as compared with 31 per cent (see Table 6.6).

TABLE 6.6 Reasons for the non-attendance by appellants at tribunal
hearings as posited by representatives* **

Reason	% of representatives stating these views
Nervousness	43.6
Work	29.7
Sickness; poor health	26.7
Appellant sees no chance of success	22.8
Frivolous appeal	11.9
Distance; transport difficulties	10
Family responsibilities	9
Apathy	8.9
Appealed in frustration	6
Appellant is elderly	3
Other or additional reasons given	19.8

*   Totals add to more than 100 per cent (N=101) since many respon-
     dents gave more than one answer.
** Total does not agree with sample size as cases where there is no
     information are exluded.

THE NEED FOR ADVICE

It must be borne in mind that this study is concerned with 'welfare'
tribunals, and because of this the social background to many of the
appeals is one of acute stress; the right to one's home may be
threatened, an appellant may be sick or unemployed and unexpectedly
be refused benefit, or he or she may have been struggling for years
to manage on supplementary benefit allowances. In such cases the
appeal is likely to have been motivated by a general sense of injustice, desperation and deprivation relating to the appellant's
whole life situation, rather than to an issue which falls neatly

into a specific category of appeal. A person who applies to the
Rent Tribunal may really be trying to force the landlord into carrying out essential repairs because the conditions under which the
family is living may be causing overcrowding (if certain rooms cannot be used), and health problems. On the other hand, the applicant
may be using the appeal as a means of controlling the activities of
other tenants rather than asking for a rent reduction. Yet because
only the issue of rent or security come within the jurisdiction of
the tribunal, the chairman is often heard leading the applicant back
to what, for the tribunal, is the central issue. A similarly wide
spectrum of 'needs' may equally apply to a deserted wife or to a
permanently injured man appearing before Supplementary Benefit or
National Insurance Tribunals. Both will be concerned with their
total life situation and with the very wide ramifications of their
overall position in society. (9)

All groups agreed - appellants, chairmen and members, and representatives - that it was very useful for an appellant to take advice
before going along to the hearing. The two latter categories tended
to think that the Citizens Advice Bureau was the best agency for
appellants to approach, whereas the appellants themselves were likely
to choose a more specific source, one which they perceived as being
more directly related to the nature of their immediate problem. (10)
Table 6.7 shows the actual sources of advice used by appellants in
our sample.

TABLE 6.7 Agencies approached for advice prior to a hearing according to type of tribunal*

Agency	% of appellants who sought advice		
	NILTs	SBATs	RTs
Solicitor	16.3	4.4	42.1
Trade union	34.9	4.4	-
Citizens Advice Bureau	14	2.2	21.1
LA Social Services Dept	-	17.8	-
Voluntary group	14	42	15.8
Claimants Union	2.1	13.3	-
Friends or relatives	4.7	6.7	15.8
Other or additional agency	16.3	8.9	15.8
Total	(N=43)	(N=45)	(N=19)

* Totals may exceed 100 per cent because more than one source of
  advice was often mentioned.

From the above table it will be noted that only about half of
the appellants interviewed took advice before going to the hearing
and, as might be expected, there were considerable differences with
regard to the type of agency approached depending upon the type of
tribunal. The largest number of National Insurance appellants said

that they turned to their trade union, the next preferred adviser
being a solicitor. Rent Tribunal applicants tended to go to a
solicitor first and were also more likely to have approached the
Citizens Advice Bureau. Supplementary Benefits appellants had
mainly turned to voluntary agencies, welfare rights groups and
advice centres, and were also more likely to have approached social
services departments.

Of those who sought advice from all these varied sources, 68 per
cent found it helpful, and judging by these responses, it seems that
current provisions are tending to meet the early advisory needs of
those appellants who use them. However, it appears that consultation and encouragement may be very necessary at this stage, since
8.5 per cent of National Insurance appellants and 14 per cent of
Supplementary Benefits appellants said that they had been discouraged from appealing, and in some instances claimed they were
intimidated by threats and bribes. In the case of Supplementary
Benefits appellants, three quarters of these particular appellants
said they were discouraged by their local office, the figure in the
case of National Insurance appellants being somewhat lower – less
than half – the remainder said they were discouraged in the main by
friends. Whilst we cannot substantiate these claims in any way it
would seem that there is some cause for concern since they were made
by interviewees having no personal acquaintance with each other and
coming from different geographical areas and hence referring to
different offices.

The Legal Advice and Assistance Act 1972 allows an appellant to a
tribunal to receive advice from a solicitor about his case and about
tribunal procedure prior to a hearing under the Legal Aid Scheme
(known as the £25 scheme). However, our analysis of interviews
indicated that 78 per cent of all appellants claimed they had never
heard of this provision at all and did not know that they might be
entitled to legal help in respect of tribunal appeal. It is, therefore, hardly surprising that the Law Society commented recently that:
'A cause of disappointment to us is that no more than about 1 per
cent of all applications for payment have been in respect of tribunal
problems.' (12)

There is no doubt that, once approached, some solicitors, as well
as voluntary agencies and legal advice centres, did inform appellants
of their rights under the scheme, and a very small number of those
interviewed had in fact made use of the provision. Most of them had
heard of, or seen, the scheme mentioned in the media, or had seen
leaflets at advisory centres or in public offices. However, even
this small group was for the most part either ill-informed or mis-
informed. Some admitted to not really knowing what was involved,
others thought that the advice service did not apply to tribunals,
and yet others confused advice with representation. When, as
researchers, we were asked to explain how the scheme worked, the
general response was very favourable, though some appellants pointed
out that advice alone would be useless unless a representative also
appeared at the hearing.

As many as 13 per cent of the non-legal representatives had not
heard of the scheme; those who had done so favoured its extension
to include representation. Of the chairmen and members, those with
legal qualifications expressed more favourable views towards the

scheme than did non-lawyers, though this was somewhat half-hearted and there was no general enthusiasm for extending legal aid to cover representation.

VIEWS ABOUT REPRESENTATION

Appellants

Of the appellants interviewed, 28 per cent of Rent Tribunal applicants were represented, 46 per cent of National Insurance Local
Tribunal appellants and 53 per cent of Supplementary Benefits
Appeal appellants. (13) Of these, over half felt that it had had a
positive effect on the result, although over a third maintained that
it had little effect one way or the other.
  Excluding the Rent Tribunal cases (where it is difficult to define
'success' in any meaningful way), 38 per cent of those who were
represented and whom we interviewed had the decision reversed in
their favour, whereas this was true of only 17 per cent of those not
represented. People seemed well aware that representation was a
complex matter and that its effect was not a straightforward one:

  'It's a great help to have a representative to present the case,
  but if he weren't there, they might be more sympathetic. If I'd
  gone by myself with such a case they might have said, it's your
  fault, why didn't you get someone to help you.'

Many commented that it gave them moral support rather than affecting the decision.
  A large proportion of the unrepresented appellants - again excluding Rent Tribunal cases - felt that they would have had a better
chance had they been represented, but many of these had not known
how to set about finding someone, or they were confused by the word-
ing of the tribunal papers:

  'I think they should give you one automatically, not make it hard
  to find. An ordinary person doesn't know lawyers.'

  'On the letter you weren't allowed a solicitor, you could just
  take a friend.'

  Both represented and unrepresented claimed that the result was
as they had expected but whereas the unrepresented appellants tended
to do worse than they hoped, appellants who were represented more
often commented that they did better than they had hoped. There
were two other important differences between appellants, according
to whether or not they were represented, reflecting differences
in their subjective assessments of the tribunal situation. First,
represented appellants more often stated that they had felt
nervous or worried at the prospect of the hearing. They may have
felt that there was a lot at stake and had therefore obtained a
representative to put the case across for them. Second, represented
appellants more often commented that the tribunal had been 'fair'
to them. Those unrepresented people who felt that they had been

unfairly treated identified their complaints as undue haste in the
proceedings and unfairness in skilful advocacy. Decisions were regarded as 'unfair' when the appellant thought his request was both
realistic and necessary, for example, a Supplementary Benefits
appellant whose rent was £10 per week received only £7 per week on
the grounds that this was reasonable for the area. Such a decision
ignored the question of scarcity and was viewed by the appellant
as unjust. Another example concerned a man whose unemployment disqualification was reduced from six to three weeks, but he felt it
unfair that he should have been disqualified at all.

The following quotations from interviews give some idea of
appellants' attitudes towards their experience of representation:

National Insurance Appellant:
   'Very important - I wouldn't have fancied going up on my own.
   I couldn't have explained the rules and regulations of the docks.
   But the case was disallowed. A legal man that knew the docks may
   have been more helpful, may have put the case better. The
   Chairman is a legal fellow and might have been impressed by a
   legal person.' (Represented by a Union Official)

Supplementary Benefits Appellant:
   'Yes, I think the message was put over quite well. It did help to
   have someone representing who can speak because I get depression
   and might break down.' (Represented by Local Authority Social
   Worker)

   'A social worker came with me, we both did our bit - I did most
   of the talking, she was there and put her spoke in when someone
   said what they shouldn't, sucn as when the presenting officer
   said that with bronchitis, a cold bedroom is best!'(Represented
   by Local Authority Social Worker)

National Insurance Appellant:
   'Mr X got all the medical evidence together and wrote to them....
   It's 90 per cent presentation of case. He wouldn't go in until
   all his facts were ready. Me, with that fellow (Insurance
   Officer) I'd have been tied up by words, if I was by myself.'
   (Represented by a Union Official)

Rent Applicant:
   'It gave us moral support rather than affected the decision. I
   knew the landlord was getting advice, it helped us to have someone there.'

On the whole the attitudes of the appellants toward representation were quite positive although they held very varied expectations
of the representatives' role, ranging from emotional support to
complex legal skills. It seemed clear that many more appellants
would take advantage of advisory and representational services if
only they know where and how to obtain them, especially if they were
made free. Lack of information as to who to approach was mentioned
by very many appellants. Seventy per cent of those who attended
the hearing did so unaccompanied. When they were also unrepresented

their recollection of the proceedings centred on their fears and
general vulnerability rather than on the specific details of the
case. Many said they were very nervous and would have welcomed ex-
planations concerning what was happening, but these were not forthcoming from the tribunal members. Representatives were thought to
be desirable as interpreters and to bridge the social divide between
appellants and tribunal members, as well as providing legal skills.

Once having appeared before a tribunal, appellants' views concerning sources of advice and representation changed somewhat.
Forty-one per cent of Rent Tribunal applicants said that in any
similar situation in the future they would not want a representative, presumably because they felt that their interests had been
protected without one. Of those who would have liked to be represented, the largest number (38 per cent) said that they would want
a lawyer. The rest mentioned people from Housing Aid and Advice
Centres or the possibility of help from Shelter and similar organisations. Thirty-six per cent of National Insurance appellants
opted for a solicitor or barrister as a preferred representative,
with 27 per cent stating that they would go to their union. Of
these, quite a number specifically stated that it must be a union
'solicitor' and not just any official.

Supplementary Benefits appellants were more divided in their
opinions as to who could provide the best representation, and tended
to indicate their preference for people from non-statutory agencies,
like Citizens Rights, CHECK! (Liverpool only), Free Representation
Unit, (14) Task Force, or a legal service such as that provided by
a Neighbourhood Law Centre. Whatever the agency selected, the view

TABLE 6.8 Appellants' views on the best type of representative at a
tribunal hearing* **

Representative	NILTs % appellants	SBATs % appellants	RTs % appellants
Would not want to be represented	13.8	14.9	41
Solicitor or barrister	37.3	18.1	38.5
Trade union	26.7	1.1	-
Social Services	1.1	14.9	2.6
CHECK!	5.3	13.9	-
Claimants Union	-	4.3	-
Housing Aid/Shelter	-	1.1	5.1
Other	14.9	35.1	23.1
Don't know	7.4	5.3	2.6
Total	(N=94)	(N=94)	(N=39)

* Totals exceed 100 per cent since respondents often mentioned more
   than one type of representative.
** Totals may not agree with sample size since cases where there is
   no information are excluded.

was always prefaced by the statement that the service must be 'free',
as most Supplementary Benefit appellants could not afford to contribute anything. Eighteen per cent mentioned a solicitor or barrister
as most desirable, and a further 15 per cent opted for the local
authority social service department (for details see Table 6.8).

It is noteworthy that the statutory agencies do not seem to inspire much confidence in relation to the provision of representation.
Legally trained professionals or workers from a voluntary agency
not closely identifiable with any bureaucratic system were the
preferred groups. In respect of social workers, this is perhaps
particularly unfortunate because their influence, particularly on
the Supplementary Benefits Tribunal, can be considerable and their
evidence is weighed seriously·by the members if they are convinced
of the social worker's knowledge and interest. (15)

Chairmen and members

The attitudes of chairmen and members towards representation were
highly ambivalant. Although three quarters of them felt that there
were in fact advantages to an appellant being represented, since
the effective presentation of a case would make for clarity, relevance, precision and an economic use of time, about half of these
same people went on to point out that tribunal deliberations were
not affected by representation, nor would the outcome for the
appellant be affected by it! These contradicting statements were
not adequately clarified, but their general view was that they did
not think that representation affected the way the appellant was
treated, but conceded that he or she probably felt more at ease if
represented.

Welfare or Citizens Rights Groups, particularly the Claimants
Union, were shrugged off as having little or no effect on tribunal decisions, though our observations at hearings tended not to
confirm this. The antagonism which flares when appellants or their
representatives adopt a conflict position is usually skated over in
rational discussion, but we witnessed less sedate and more dis-
comfited struggles at actual hearings. At times, the efforts of
such groups forced a tribunal to make a decision based on adherence
to the 'law' and 'rights', rather than relying on their discretionary powers and arbitrary benevolence. The above refers specifically
to Supplementary Benefit hearings, but trade union representatives
appearing before National Insurance hearings are sometimes viewed
in a similarly 'troublesome' light, although members are wary of
their skilled advocacy in matters of industrial and national
insurance law, as well as their undoubted political backing. By
contrast, social workers are viewed by tribunal members in a
positive light in so far as they adopt an advisory or supportive
role towards the appellant.

In nearly all the areas explored, the Supplementary Benefits
chairmen and members held the least favourable opinons with reference to representation. They were more adamant that representation
had little positive effect than were similar groups in other types
of tribunal and they were the most strongly opposed to representation by people from Rights Groups. More of them were opposed to the

£25 scheme and to the idea of extending Legal Aid to representation
before tribunals. We believe that these attitudes reflect many
of the characteristics pertaining to members of Supplementary
Benefits Tribunals and which were discussed earlier: lack of training, little detailed knowledge of the legislation, a predilection
for 'character judgment' and a failure to consider in any detail the
complex definitions of concepts affecting the entitlement. Undoubtedly, such factors increase their resistance to the potentially
clarifying effects of legal representation; they may fear that the
legal skills of representation will be used to challenge the way
discretionary powers are used and to point out the inconsistencies
in decision-making as between comparable cases.

THE FUTURE FOR REPRESENTATION

It is not intended to say much about the role of representation
before the Rent Tribunal in view of the changes in jurisdiction
brought about by the 1974 Rent Act. We did not observe any hearings subsequent to the passing of the new Act nor did we interview
anyone who had taken a case before such a tribunal under the new
legislation. There are fears that since privately rented furnished
premises where the landlord is not resident have now become protected
by statute under the same provisions as unfurnished premises, those
premises which remain unprotected may be the focus of a bitter
struggle between landlord and tenant as the supply of accommodation
available to rent shrinks. Concern has also been expressed lest
landlords try to bypass the security provisions of the Act by claiming some exceptional circumstances, such as the provision of 'board'
or the description of the premises as 'holiday lettings'. If
circumstances such as these arise, representation on behalf of unprotected tenants may become crucial, particularly that undertaken
by those with legal skills.
    National Insurance appellants have established a pattern of look-
ing to the unions and to lawyers for representational help. This
has been the most logical development due to the fact that a system
of precedent is referred to in decision-making and the chairman of
the tribunal is a lawyer who often has a tendency to conduct hearings with courtlike formality. Those union officials who appear on
behalf of appellants tend to specialise in representation and are
knowledgeable over a wide area of industrial and some welfare law,
as well as being skilled in handling the types of disputes involved.
Their role on behalf of the appellant is almost the exact counter-
part of the Insurance Officer's role on behalf of the department.
Kathleen Bell (16) has shown that their contribution is very effective in terms of a favourable outcome, and our observations, as well
as the comments of appellants, would tend to confirm this. As was
pointed out earlier, appellants showed some preference for a
solicitor specialising in trade union matters.
    There is, however, one important factor to be borne in mind: of
all the National Insurance Tribunal appellants interviewed, fewer
than a quarter were unionised and able to call upon their officials
for assistance. Furthermore, although we have no hard data to
support the criticism, it was suggested to us that union officials

can be quite selective in the cases they will accept for representation.

For the non-unionised the main alternative would appear to be improved access to legal representation, though the need to deal sensitively with areas of personal and social stress would seem to argue for a rather new type of advocate. For this purpose too, some contact system which would direct people to experienced sources of help would be essential.

Representation before Supplementary Benefit Tribunals raises more complex questions regarding the effectiveness of various types of representation. The needs and preferences of the appellant have to be weighed against the attitudes of tribunal members towards different groups who offer representation. According to national statistics, (17) the most effective type of representation in terms of increased awards is provided by the CPAG (66.7 per cent) followed by social workers (54.7 per cent) and the Claimants Union (46.1 per cent). Trade union officials and even friends and relatives are more effective than solicitors (see Table B.3, Appendix B). It seems that despite a considerable amount of open hostility towards civil rights groups, and claims that their presence at times acted against the interest of the appellant, they appear to be effective in achieving a positive outcome for the appellant. Social workers, too, are shown by these statistics to be less ineffectual than both appellants and some tribunal chairmen and members think they are. The problem is that representation by these smaller groups forms only a tiny proportion of all representation before Supplementary Benefits Tribunals and it might be claimed that their success rate is a reflection of the way in which they select cases. However, interviews with all those representatives at Supplementary Benefit Tribunals who were attached to civil rights groups indicated that many of them would often appeal as a matter of principle and even if there was little chance of success, simply in order to make the point about their clients' circumstances. Usually it was claimed that if the case appeared poor but the appellant wanted representation, they would go ahead and pursue it. This would tend to refute the argument that the high 'success' rate of this type of representation reflects any careful selectivity of 'worthwhile' cases.

National statistics indicate that in only 2.8 per cent of cases before Supplementary Benefit Tribunals is the appellant represented by a solicitor. In view of our earlier comments regarding the problems of discretionary justice which so beset tribunals of this type, it may be argued that their intervention could lead to a proper definition of policy, and clarification of the rules upon which an appellant may base his case. The advantages for the client inherent in such a situation may well outweigh the disadvantages of legalism, but, as was mentioned earlier, for the intervention of lawyers to be a meaningful alternative, legal aid, widespread publicity and an explicit means of putting appellants in touch with lawyers would need to be available.

In the long term, however, it must be recognised that whoever engages in representation, this alone will not resolve the problem faced by the citizen appearing before an administrative tribunal - in particular a welfare tribunal. His problems are often a reflection of his economic and social circumstances and an appearance

before a tribunal can only relate to one particular aspect of his
social situation at a specific point in time. To view the solution
to these problems solely in terms of welfare benefits is to individu-
alise their nature and to deny that much deprivation and poverty is
rooted in the economic system. In lieu of wider changes however,
and if the prevailing attitude is that individuals are to be identified as the agents of their own misfortune and the source of their
own salvation, there would seem little justification for denying
them at least the right to free representation before tribunals.

Chapter 7

SOME CONCLUDING COMMENTS

The present study - one of a number concerned with 'unmet legal need' - started from the premise that to be meaningful, any dis- cussion of the need for representation in tribunals must take full account of the context within which such representation takes place. On the basis of certain predefined criteria we therefore selected three different types of 'welfare' tribunal, and carried out a broad review of their operation both in theory and in practice. The vari- ables which it was thought were likely to be most significant in differentiating between tribunals related to the make-up and exper- tise of tribunal membership, the use of discretion or precedent in decision-making, and the extent to which the tribunal operated in- dependently of departmental influence. (1)

In carrying out the research, we have attempted to describe the social processes at work in the tribunal setting, concentrating on the interaction between the various participants in the situation: appellants, tribunal chairmen and members, representatives, and de- partmental officials. Data derived from observations at tribunal hearings and from extensive in-depth interviewing, have been set against information based on national and regional statistics. Whilst we recognise that such a method tends to 'fall between two stools', hopefully it makes some contribution to resolving the qualitative/quantitative dichotomy. (2)

The concept of 'need' as experienced by those who appeal to welfare tribunals is relative, not absolute. (3) Equally, the con- cept of 'need' in relation to legal representation is highly complex; whilst increased access to representation is essential, there is no easy solution to the question of how and in what circumstances this should be provided, nor to the question of who should provide it. Hopefully this small-scale study will have drawn attention to the very intricate nature of the problem, and to the fact that even if representation were to be vastly expanded, it would provide no panacea - other elements in the tribunal situation are as crucial, if not more so, if a more just system is to evolve.

The findings of the research highlight the essentially 'conflict- oriented' nature of tribunal appeals. Appellants are likely to be members of deprived or particularly vulnerable groups in society, caught up in a situation of crisis with which they are ill-

equipped to deal. Despite attempts to 'humanise' the tribunal
setting, to demystify it and to make it more informal, (4) the
individual appellant operates from a position of powerlessness and
finds himself ranged against powerful bureaucratic and private
interests. It cannot legitimately be maintained that case-hear-
ings are simply informal discussions, where the two sides come together on equal terms and the matter is arbitrated by an independent
third party. Our findings show that the social distance between the
tribunal membership and the appellant is only one facet of a
scenario which places the latter at a severe disadvantage, (5) one
which is greatly exacerbated at certain National Insurance and
Supplementary Benefit Tribunals where the influence exerted by departmental officials may be very considerable. (6)

When the situation in these two types of tribunal is contrasted
with that pertaining in Rent Tribunals, it becomes evident that something more than changes in procedural law, and increased representation, may lie at the heart of the matter, though these will remain
important goals. In Rent Tribunals, the situation is being radically
altered by means of legislative change which takes into account the
problems of a particularly vulnerable group in the housing market.
The powers of private landlords have been circumscribed by legislative action which affords greater protection to the tenant of
furnished accommodation. (7)

It is not here suggested that the majority of conflicts between
individuals and government departments in respect of welfare benefits
could be swept away in similar fashion. Nevertheless, we feel that
there are many areas of welfare which require review at the level of
social policy with a view to legislative change. Examples would
include the problems of single parents and deserted wives, particularly in relation to the cohabitation rule, and the difficulties of
large families with young children, faced by the wage-stop. We believe there is a need to take certain cases outside the domain of
tribunal adjudication and, at the same time, to clarify legislative
intention in respect of those benefits which remain subject to
dispute.

Although the tribunal system constitutes an attempt to avoid the
alleged disadvantages of a court system, the adversarial nature of
the experience persists. So long as this is the case, the role of
representation must be seen in the context of protecting the interests of individual appellants. At a theoretical level arguments
may rage about the desirability or otherwise of 'legalising' or
'judicalising' tribunals. (8) But looking at the situation in
practice, as it exists today, if justice is to be seen to be done,
the appellant is in a very weak position vis-à-vis the other pro-
tagonists and there can be no doubt that the availability of representation is crucial to him.

Equally there may be good theoretical arguments for making changes
in the extent to which discretionary powers are available to tribunals, although the extension of 'rules' may have disadvantages
too. (9) But again, this research has been concerned with the situation as it is today, with tribunals in practice, and in this context
it would seem that the greater the degree of discretionary power
available to the panel, the more essential it is that the interests
of the appellant be protected by advocacy on his behalf. Despite

protestations to the contrary from tribunal chairmen and members, we
do not agree that they are necessarily the people best able to protect such interests, nor are we convinced that the present composition and training of panel members is conducive to independent
decision-making, when presented with the specialised knowledge of
departmental officials. (10) It is neither sufficient nor fair
that panels should continue to make decisions which vitally affect
the lives of individual appellants on the basis of what are often
stereotypical images, and at times represent no more than flimsy
character judgments. Clear factual representation is needed to off-
set the potentially negative and damaging effect of such procedures
and the recent decision to extend legal aid to tribunal representation is based on widespread recognition of this need. (11)

However, the suggestion that representation is crucial says
nothing about the type of representation, an issue which was explored at some length in the report. (12) We believe that whilst
legal expertise and training can be useful in most types of tribunal
setting, many other groups, including trade union officials, social
workers and, more especially, welfare rights groups, already make an
important contribution to this work. If they are to continue to
play this role and to expand, we would argue that their effort needs
to be supported by financial backing, and for this reason we are
disappointed that the Lord Chancellor's recommendations restrict the
use of Legal Aid monies to the payment of lawyers. The type of
rigorous advocacy required must relate both to the nature of the
case under review and to the needs of the appellant, but it should
avoid legal abstraction.

At the same time, it should be noted that there is a very real
need for advice before the case ever reaches the tribunal hearing,
and, in many instances, for an adequate follow-up service. Representation, if it is to be effective, must be accompanied by widespread publicity (which would ensure that appellants are put in
touch with representatives), and by a system of support services
which enables representatives to refer cases to those best able to
help outside the tribunal setting.

As we said earlier, representation is no panacea. In many areas
of welfare, the time is ripe for a review of social policy intentions
and their clarification through legislative change. Beyond this,
there is a need to introduce reforms relating to the practical
operation of tribunals in terms of panel membership, training, administration, procedure and access to further appeal bodies. Within the
current economic and hierarchical structuring of our society, social
justice for the inarticulate and vulnerable citizen in his dealings
with bureaucracy may constitute no more than a chimera. Dependency
is debilitating, and the militant defence of social rights only
thinly upheld: (13) a fair hearing is perhaps the most that can be
expected and the least that should be offered.

APPENDICES

APPENDICES

SOCIAL CHARACTERISTICS OF APPELLANTS

TABLE A.1   Employment status of appellants and applicants*

Status	%
Employed	50.9
Unemployed	20.2
Sick	4.8
Pensioner/retired	12.3
Other	11.8
Total	100 (N=228)

* Total does not agree with sample size because one case where there is no information is excluded.

TABLE A.2   Income of appellants and applicants according to type of tribunal*

Income	NILTs % appellants	SBATs % appellants	RTs % appellants
Under £20 per week	28.2	57.9	34.2
£20 - under £40 per week	45.7	40	47.4
£40 or more	24	2.1	13.2
Unwilling to disclose	2.2	-	5.3
Total	100 (N=92)	100 (N=95)	100 (N=38)

* Totals do not agree with sample size because cases where there is no information are excluded.

TABLE A.3   Source of income of appellants and applicants according to type of tribunal*

Source	NILTs % appellants	SBATs % appellants	RTs % applicants
SB or NI payments	18.9	65.3	27
SB or NI = additional income	6.7	13.7	13.5
Wages	67.8	18.9**	51.4
Other source of income	6.6	2.1	8.1
Total	100 (N=90)	100 (N=95)	100 (N=37)

*   Totals do not agree with sample size because cases where there is no information are excluded.
** At the time of interview, some supplementary benefit applicants had resumed employment. A further two cases related to Family Income Supplement.

TABLE A.4   Household size of applicants or appellants according to type of tribunal

Household size	NILTs % appellants	SBATs % appellants	RTs % appellants
1 person	16	20.8	25.6
2 persons	25.5	19.8	25.9
3 persons	20.2	13.5	20.5
4 persons	18.1	16.7	10.3
5+ persons	20.2	29.1	7.7
Total	100 (N=94)	100 (N=96)	100 (N=39)

TABLES RELATING TO
DESCRIPTION OF REPRESENTATIVES

TABLE B.1   Agency or group from which representatives came

Agency	Representatives %
Trade union	24.5
Social worker	17.6
Solicitor's firm	15.7
CHECK!	12.7
Claimants Union	7.8
Free Representation Unit	4.9
Housing Aid/Advice Centres	3.9
Law centres	2.0
Other	10.8
Total	100 (N=103)

TABLE B.2   Legal background of representatives

Background	Representatives %
Non-lawyer	66
Solicitor	17.5
Articled clerk; legal executive	4.9
Barrister, pupil	3.8
Law student; law graduate	7.8
Total	100 (N=103)

TABLE B.3 Effectiveness of different types of representation at Supplementary Benefit Appeal Tribunals

Representative	% of total represented	% where award increased
Friend, relative	65.4	33.1
Trade union official	1.6	43.5
Solicitor	2.8	28.6
Social worker	9.4	54.7
CPAG	2	66.7
Claimants Union	13.8	46.1
Other	4.9	46.6
Total	100 (N=1477)	

Source: Table supplied by DHSS for quarter ending 31 March 1973.

TABLE B.4 Experience of different types of tribunals

Type of tribunal	Representatives %
SBATs only	24.3
NILTs only	17.5
RTs only	7.8
Combination of above	15.5
Other tribunal experience	35
Total	100 (N=103)

TABLE B.5 Length of experience with tribunals*

Length	Representatives %
Less than 1 yr	28.9
1 yr - less than 3 yrs	28.9
3 yrs - less than 10 yrs	20
10 yrs or longer	22.2
Total	100 (N=90)

* Table excludes thirteen representatives interviewed after their only tribunal representation.

TABLE B.6   Number of representations in previous year*

Number	Representatives %
Less than 5	51.1
5 - less than 10	18.2
10 - less than 25	12.5
25 - less than 50	9.1
50 or more	9.1
Total	100 (N=90)

* Table exludes thirteen representatives interviewed
after their only tribunal representation.

NOTES

FOREWORD

1 See also A. Byles and P. Morris, 'Unmet Need: The Case of the
   Neighbourhood Law Centre', Routledge & Kegan Paul, 1977. R.R.
   Anderson, 'Representation in the Context of the Juvenile Court',
   C. Grace and P. Wilkinson, 'Negotiating the Law: Legal
   Phenomena in Welfare Provision', Routledge & Kegan Paul, forthcoming.
2 Report prepared by Sir William Beveridge, 'Social Insurance and
   Allied Services', HMSO, Cmnd 6406, 1942.
3 See T.H. Marshall, 'Social Policy', Hutchinson, 1965, revised
   1970, esp. Part II.
4 The element of social control implicit in the reforms of the
   welfare state is not a relevant issue for discussion here, but
   it may be worth considering the extent to which the dependency
   relationship between state and individual was reinforced by
   such reforms.
5 See, for example, B. Abel-Smith and P. Townsend, 'The Poor and
   the Poorest', Fabian Society Pamphlet, 1965.
6 On education see for example, J.E. Floud, A.H. Halsey and F.M.
   Martin (eds), 'Social Class and Educational Opportunity',
   Heinemann, 1956 also O. Banks, 'The Sociology of Education',
   Batsford, 1968 esp. pp. 53-66. On housing see for example, D.V.
   Donnison (ed.), 'Essays on Housing', Codicote Press, 1964 and
   the Report of the Committee on Housing in Greater London
   (Milner Holland), HMSO, Cmnd 2605, 1965.
7 See P. Marris and M. Rein, 'Dilemmas of Social Reform',
   Routledge & Kegan Paul, 1967.
8 See for example, A. Sinfield, 'Which Way to Social Work', Fabian
   Society Pamphlet, 1969, and later, the introduction of the
   journal 'Case-Con'.
9 As is noted in another volume in this series of work undertaken
   by LARU, careful examination of the data shows that this is in
   fact an oversimplified account of the process of negotiation
   which takes place between social worker and client. See C.
   Grace and P. Wilkinson, op. cit.
10 These concerns had been expressed in various proposals put

forward to remedy the situation, see for example, 'Justice for All', Society of Labour Lawyers report, Fabian Research Series 273, 1968; also 'Rough Justice', Conservative Political Centre, 1968; and the recommendations of the Law Society, 'Second Memorandum on Legal Advice and Assistance', Council of the Law Society, 1969.

11 See for example P. Morris, R. White and P. Lewis, 'Social Needs and Legal Action', Martin Robertson, 1973; also E. Bridges, B. Suffrin, J. Whetton and R. White, 'Legal Services in Birmingham', University of Birmingham, Institute of Judicial Administration, 1975, esp. the Introduction.

12 It could legitimately be argued that the areas of need encompassed within the framework of legal services are decided by the government rather than by the legal profession. However, this is to ignore both the very powerful pressure that the profession is able to exert upon government, and the fact that the legislation allows the profession a high degree of discretion in determining the extent to which legal services shall be made available.

13 Undoubtedly the American Bar is more politically activist than is the case in Commonwealth countries where the legal professions may be characterised as less innovative and more conservative.

14 See chapter 1.

15 See 'Report of the Committee on Administrative Tribunals and Enquiries', HMSO, Cmnd 218, July 1957.

16 At Supplementary Benefit and National Insurance Appeal Tribunals.

17 See Hansard, House of Lords, 19 June 1976, cols 1211 onwards, particularly col. 1215.

18 Under this scheme appellants may take advice about tribunal hearings from a lawyer, written reports may be prepared for them and on occasion, lawyers have appeared as advisers rather than as direct advocates under the 'McKenzie' ruling. The latter, however, is a rare occurrence.

19 Theoretically tribunals are intended to be inquisitorial in nature, but in practice tend to adopt an adversarial approach.

CHAPTER 1   PLANNING THE RESEARCH

1 P. Morris, 'Unmet Need: Initial Considerations', unpublished paper, 1971.

2 Theoretical and methodological reasons for selecting these particular welfare tribunals are discussed in chapter 2.

3 'Department of Health and Social Security Annual Report 1973', HMSO, Cmnd 5706, July 1974, p. 86.

4 Ibid., p. 88.

5 Medical, surgical, optical, aural or dental requirements were excluded from the supplementary Benefit Act 1966 with effect from 1 November 1974 (SI, no. 1191 (c.22) of 1974).

6 'Report of the Interdepartmental Committee on Rent Control', HMSO, Cmnd 6621, 1945.

7 'Social Trends', no. 4, Central Statistical Office, HMSO, 1973 p. 174.

8   Phillip Pearson, 'A New Deal for Furnished Tenants', Shelter, 1973.
9   See, for example, Melvin Herman, 'Administrative Justice and Supplementary Benefits' Occasional Papers on Social Administration, no. 47, 1971; T. Lynes, 'Welfare Rights', Fabian Tract 395, 1969.
10 'Annual Report of the Council on Tribunals', 1971/2.
11 'Legal Aid and Advice, Report of the Law Society, and Comments and Recommendations of the Lord Chancellor's Advisory Committee 1972/3' (twenty-third report), HMSO, 1973.
12 'Legal Aid and Advice, Report of the Law Society, and Comments and Recommendations of the Lord Chancellor's Advisory Committee 1973/4' (twenty-fourth report), HMSO, 1974.

CHAPTER 2   THE STUDY

1   This point is illustrated in a later section, where the problem of 'access' to study local tribunals is discussed.
2   For a more detailed discussion of the findings of this Committee see chapter 3.
3   Comparative rates of unemployment:

North west	2.9%	Greater London	1.5%
Merseyside	6.9%	Gravesend	2.2%
Liverpool	7.3%		
Chester	3.1%		

Source: Department of Employment Gazette, August 1974
4   Source: 1971 census.
5   All research workers involved in this project were required to sign the Official Secrets Act.
6   For a detailed breakdown according to type of tribunal, see tables 2.4, 2.5 and 2.6.
7   C.A. Moser and G. Kalton, 'Survey Methods in Social Investigation', Heinemann, 1971.
8   This discussion cannot be extended to applicants at Rent Tribunals, since we do not have the necessary information. These applicants constitute a smaller proportion of the whole.
9   See chapter 6, note 7.
10 In only one case did a research worker have to abandon an interview carried out in a pub. Another interview, with an appellant suffering from severe palsy, was also abandoned when the research worker decided it was more important to help get him rehoused.
11 For further details, see also Appendix A and Tables 2.1-2.4.
12 Social class here refers to the 5 point classification employed by the Registrar-General (UK General Register Office, 1966). It is based on the occupation held by the respondent. In the case of retired or unemployed respondents, the classification was based on former occupation. Table 2.9 condenses the categories for brevity.
13 These comparisons relate only to data from observations, which covered random samples of cases. The sample of appellants, being based on selected groups of represented and non-represented cases, is not typical of all appellants.

14   See 'Social Work Today', vol. 4, no. 6, 14 June 1973, p. 186.
15   Often referred to as a 'Hawthorne effect', see F.J.
     Roethlisberger and W.J. Dickson, 'Management and the Worker',
     Harvard University Press, 1939.
16   See also Kathleen Bell, 'Research Study on Supplementary Benefit
     Appeal Tribunals. Review of Main Findings: Conclusions:
     Recommendations', HMSO, 1975, for similar findings.

CHAPTER 3   TO FRANKS AND AFTER

1   See R.E. Wraith and P.G. Hutchesson, 'Administrative Tribunals',
    Allen & Unwin, 1973, for a comprehensive discussion of the
    origins and development of administrative tribunals, particu-
    larly chapter 1.
2   'Such cases had occupied an increasing proportion of the time of
    the courts and had involved both employers and trade unions in
    substantial costs.' (p. 258);   'Cases had to wait over six months
    before they were heard.' (p. 116) - B. Abel-Smith and P. Stevens,
    'Lawyers and the Courts', Heinemann, 1967.
3   'Report of the Donoughmore Committee', HMSO, Cmnd 4060, April
    1932 (reprinted 1966).
4   For a brief resume of the issue, see K. Bell, 'Tribunals in the
    Social Services', Routledge & Kegan Paul, 1969, p. 16.
5   'Report of the Committee on Administrative Tribunals and En-
    quiries', HMSO, Cmnd 218, July 1957.
6   Wraith and Hutchesson, op. cit., p. 41.
7   Ibid., p. 40.
8   For a full discussion of the Franks Committee recommendations,
    see Bell, op. cit., pp. 22-3.
9   For a discussion of how members are nominated to panels, see
    chapter 4.
10 See chapter 6.
11 'Report of the Committee on Administrative Tribunals and En-
    quiries', p. 19, para. 77.
12 Public sympathy is rarely extended to landlords, unless they are
    of very limited means and in difficult circumstances themselves.
13 In the present study, they were never asked to withdraw.
14 At one particular hearing, the clerk warned the tribunal members
    that the next appellant was a member of the Claimants Union who
    had 'illegally' employed a tape-recorder to record a conversation
    with a social security officer.   It was decided to ask the young
    man to leave his coat outside, or remove it, to prevent a similar
    re-occurrence.   A very long and challenging hearing ensued after
    which the young man 'lost' his case;   he was, however, applauded
    for 'livening up the proceedings'.
15 For example, reasons for decisions of SBATs often took the form:
        The Commissions decision is upheld as the appellants require-
        ments and resources are considered to be reasonably assessed
        in accordance with the Acts and Regulations and the tribunal
        can find no grounds upon which it would be appropriate to ex-
        ercise the discretionary powers therein contained.
16 'Report of the Committee on Administrative Tribunals and En-
    quiries, para. 38, p.9.

17 Since the implementation of the 1974 Rent Act we are informed that waiting time has been reduced to three weeks in these tribunals (private communication, October 1974).

18 DHSS has commented that for SBATs at least, 76.5 per cent of appeals were heard in under 4 weeks (91.5 per cent in less than six weeks).

19 DHSS pointed out that some of the reasons for delay relate to appellants, e.g. seeking adjournments due to inability to attend; failure to be available for further interview when a tribunal has adjourned a case for further information.

20 See, for example, Wraith and Hutchesson, op. cit., p. 259.

21 The majority of those interviewed in the present research were legally qualified, however.

22 The extent to which this makes the tribunal dependent upon the expertise of Department officials will be discussed later.

23 H. Street, 'Justice in the Welfare State', Stevens, 1968, p. 5.

24 See, J. Fulbrook, R. Brooke and P. Archer, 'Tribunals: A Social Court?' Fabian Tract 427, December 1973, pp. 4-5. A provincial appellant may not be aware that these are available to be consulted, and might in any case find travelling to London too expensive. (DHSS, in answer to this criticism, has commented that unpublished decisions are ordinarily available to members of the public at the Commissioners headquarters in London, and also at their Edinburgh and Cardiff offices. In the opinion of the Commissioners these unpublished decisions, which follow established principles are not regarded as being of interest or importance outside the particular case. Other interested parties might argue that this situation works to the disadvantage of the provinical appellant and DHSS official).

25 Phillip Pearson, 'A New Deal for Furnished Tenants', Shelter, 1973, p. 13.

26 'Report of the Committee on Administrative Tribunals and Enquiries', para. 64, p. 15.

27 The question of non-attendance will be discussed in more detail in a subsequent chapter.

28 See, for example, Bell, op. cit., Street, op. cit. and M. Herman, 'Administrative Justice and Supplementary Benefits', Occasional Papers on Social Administration, no. 47, Bell, 1972. Also, publications of the Child Poverty Action Group and the more official comments of the Council on Tribunals and the Lord Chancellor's Advisory Committee on Legal Aid and Advice.

29 See review and discussion by Ruth Lister of, 'Tribunals: A Social Court?' in 'Poverty', (Journal of the Child Poverty Action Group) no. 29, Summer 1974, pp. 46ff.

CHAPTER 4 THE INDEPENDENCE OF TRIBUNALS

1 'Report of the Committee on Administrative Tribunals and Enquiries', HMSO, Cmnd 218, July, 1957, p. 15, para. 64.

2 See W.E. Cavenagh and D. Newton, Administrative Tribunals: How People Become Members, 'Public Administration', summer 1971, pp. 198-200, for a detailed account of how appointments are made to Rent Tribunals.

3 Justices of the Peace are likewise only selected from a very
   small section of the community. Only 15 per cent are wage-
   earners and 71 per cent are either non-employed, professional
   men or employers. R. Hood, 'Sentencing in Magistrates' Courts',
   Stevens, 1969.
4 See discussion, chapter 1.
5 The maximum compensation was increased to £8 per day on 1 December 1975.
6 The figure of 73 per cent contrasts with the findings of a
   survey of NILTs in Scotland and Northern England which showed
   that 64 per cent of the employee's panels and 25 per cent of the
   employer's panels were not in social classes I and II. See
   Kathleen Bell, et. al. National Insurance Local Tribunals: 'A
   Research Study Journal of Social Policy, vol. 3, part 4, 19XX p. 313.
7 See Cavenagh and Newton, op. cit., pp. 200, 201, 213 for a very
   similar breakdown on the sources of tribunal membership. Also,
   Ruth Lister, 'Justice for the Claimant', The Membership Child
   Poverty Action Group, 1974, p. 7, for a very similar conclusion.
   'Clearly, present recruitment policies lead to a membership neither
   representative of claimants nor in close touch with their problems'.
8 'Report of the Committee on Administrative Tribunals and Enquiries', p. 61.
9 Melvin Herman, 'Administrative Justice and Supplementary
   Benefits', Occasional Papers on Social Administration, no. 47,
   Bell, 1972, p. 23.
10 One SBAT clerk commented to a research worker after a session
   'You don't take notes on the clerk, do you? (laugh). What I
   say, well, sometimes the tribunal needs a little help - well -
   we get messages from above to behave ourselves (laugh).'
11 At a session of a different SBAT, the clerk, although mainly
   silent during the hearing, was observed to make suggestions and
   gave possible decisions to the tribunal during the deliberations
   following all six cases heard. He was not challenged by the
   tribunal. The following example of his role is extracted from the
   research worker's field notes. 'Clerk argued stongly that (the
   tribunal) can't pay squatters as householders, (their) expenses
   (are) not so great. Can't oppose this principle - only give
   allowance if there is a responsibility for rent. Clerk very
   dominant, never stopped talking.'
12 As suggested by J. Fulbrook and P. Archer in 'Tribunals: A
   Social Court?', Fabian Tract 427, December 1973, p. 10.
13 Herman, op. cit., p. 28.
14 See 'Annual Report of the Council on Tribunals', 1972/3, p. 21.
15 Insurance officers appearing at local tribunals are not
   necessarily engaged full time on Insurance officer duties.
16 During a case involving the wage-stop, where the appellant was
   absent the presenting officer commented that the appellant 'had
   £47 rent arrears which shows he was misusing public funds'.
17 One example concerns the occasion when a West Indian woman with
   two children appealing on the issue of FIS payments was asked
   whether the same father was responsible for both children.
18 At one NILT the official 'commented to an appellant who had left
   employment in a canteen after only one day's work there. 'As a
   married woman I would have thought you would be used to
   kitchen work and preparation.'

CHAPTER 5 THE USE OF DISCRETION

1 H. Street, 'Justice in the Welfare State', Stevens, 1968, p. 8.
2 Paul Harrison, The Tribunals of the Welfare State, 'New Society', 22 November 1973.
3 Henry Hodge, Techniques for Tribunals - 1, 'Legal Action Group Bulletin', December 1973, p. 271.
4 DHSS has commented that:
   the question whether a claimant has shown good cause, e.g. for delay in claiming benefit, requires a SUBJECTIVE rather than an objective approach, having regard to a claimant's age, state of health, previous experience, access to information, and so forth. Claimants may differ widely in any or all of these respects, so that it is by no means inconsistent to find that, in otherwise identical circumstances one claimant shows good cause while another does not. (Emphasis added)
5 For example, in respect of appeals against the six-week disqualification of benefits rule in cases of voluntary unemployment.
6 See Roger Gomm, The Claimant as Mendicant, 'Social Work Today', vol. 5, no. 12, 19 September 1974, for a description of attitudes adopted by claimants of social security in uneasy defence of their position.
7 David Bull in, Living Beneath the Clothes Line, 'Guardian', 7 December 1973, gives examples of the failure of local offices to follow the internal instructions of the SBC in respect of Form B/0 40 in determining what is 'reasonable' in awarding exceptional needs payments. Determined representation by the CPAG achieved a legitimate ENP payment of £317.54 for a family whereas the average ENP payment by the Commission is only £9.55 and only one payment in 50 exceeds £20.
8 The four-week rule was suspended by the Commission in December 1973 because of the three-day week and finally abandoned in June 1974, 'because certain aspects of the rule gave rise to difficulties and sometimes led to the rule being wrongly applied'. The wage-stop was abolished in June 1975 'because the people affected (6,000) were the largest families, with the highest commitments and with the poorest prospects of the breadwinner finding suitable employment'. (Source: DHSS official.)
   The cohabitation rule, however, is to be retained. 'Guardian', 5 February 1976.
10 'Department of Health and Social Security Annual Report 1973', p. 82.
11 Ibid., p. 83.
12 The Annual Report of the Council on Tribunals for 1972/3 stated that many complaints were still being received stating that the SB tribunals were not adequately recording reasons leading to decisions. A letter was circulated to tribunal chairmen providing guidelines for setting out adequate reasons, but in our experience reasons are still given largely in terms of standard formulae without referring to individual issues.
13 See for example Henry Hodge, Welfare Law - Techniques for Tribunals, 'LAG Bulletin', December 1973, p. 270.
14 Ibid., p. 271.

15   In the determination as to whether a tenancy was furnished or
     not, the amount of rent fairly attributable to the use of furni-
     ture, on legal precedent could vary between 8 per cent and 23 per
     cent. Philip Pearson, 'A New Deal for Furnished Tenants',
     Shelter, 1974.

16   'Rent Act 1968', HMSO, chapter 23, part IV, 46(1), p. 29.

17   Pearson, op. cit., p. 3. According to the Shelter London Rent
     Tribunals survey carried out in January 1973, tenants making
     their first application for security following NTQ, were likely
     to receive an average peiod of 3.9 months.

18   Local solicitors told the researchers that the bed and breadfast
     system was abusing the rights of many of the often older, single
     and retired people living in boarding houses, Landlords would
     be pleased to give them low winter rates to ensure a steady in-
     come and then expect to be able to evict boarders during the
     summer season and charge much higher rates. This aspect of the
     problem was lost in the welter of legal tangles at this specific
     hearing and the comment of the disappointed Miss D's solicitor
     at the end was 'its been a jolly good fight anyway'. This type
     of tenancy remains unprotected under the new 1974 Rent Act.

19   This type of 'tenancy' would now be protected under the terms
     of the new 1974 Rent Act.

20   Melvin Herman, 'Administrative Justice and Supplementary
     Benefits', Occasional Papers on Social Administration, no. 47,
     Bell, 1972.

21   Ibid., p. 40.

22   Ibid., p. 43.

23   J. Fulbrook, R. Brooke and P. Archer, 'Tribunals: A Social
     Court?', Fabian Tract 427, December 1973.

24   Richard Titmuss, Welfare 'Rights', Law and Discretion, 'Political
     Quarterly', April 1971. His thesis is basically pro-discretion
     and against the frustrating legal mystification of decision-
     making via the courts.

25   Kenneth Culp Davis, 'Discretionary Justice', University of
     Illinois Press, 1971. By contrast, his thesis is that the formu-
     lation of legal rules does not completely curtail the scope of
     discretion and that it is better to confine and structure its
     extent than to leave excessive discretion unchecked.

26   Fulbrook, Brooke and Archer, op. cit., p. 16. In supporting
     this argument we do not agree, on pragmatic grounds, with their
     general thesis calling for a 'social court'.

CHAPTER 6   THE ROLE OF REPRESENTATION

1   See, for example, Kathleen Bell, Advice, Assistance and Repre-
    sentation Before Tribunals, University of Birmingham Conference
    Paper, April 1974; Melvin Herman, 'Administrative Justice and
    Supplementary Benefits', Occasional Papers on Social Administra-
    tion, no. 47, Bell, 1972. J. Fulbrook, R. Brooke and P. Archer,
    'Tribunals: A Social Court?', Fabian Tract 427, December 1973.
    'Report of the Law Society and Comments and Recommendations of
    the Lord Chancellor's Advisory Committee' 1973/4 (twenty-fourth
    report), HMSO, 1974.

2 The 'Legal Aid and Advice Report of the Law Society and
   Comments and Recommendations of the Lord Chancellor's Advisory
   Committee 1973/4 recommends that Legal Aid before tribunals
   should only be available for representation by qualified
   lawyers. This opinion conflicts with submissions made to the
   Committee by Check Rights Centre, Child Poverty Action Group,
   Free Representation Unit, Legal Action Group and the Legal
   Advice Research Unit to the effect that lay representation
   should also be covered by Legal Aid provisions.
3 See Appendix B, Tables B.1 - B.6, describing source, training
   and experience of representatives.
4 Kathleen Bell in her University of Birmingham conference paper
   points out similarly that, 'There is no doubt of the overriding
   importance of attendance', p. 39, but goes on to point out that
   the relationship to representation is close because 'attendance
   in represented cases was much higher than the average'. See
   also Herman op cit., p. 34, for a discussion of the differential
   positive effects of attendance and types of representation at
   Supplementary Benefits Appeal Tribunals.
5 Herman, op. cit., p. 37.
6 Although all appellants are entitled to claim expenses, not all
   are aware of this and only 73 per cent of those interviewed were
   offered their expenses.
7 For example, we interviewed non-attenders who had serious heart
   complaints, were stone deaf or on the verge of a nervous breakdown.
8 See Julian Fulbrook, 'The Appellant and His Case', Poverty Research Series, CPAG, 1975, for a confirmation of the economic,
   medical and psychological reasons why some appellants find
   difficulty in attending hearings.
9 See P. Morris, R. White and P. Lewis, 'Social Needs and Legal
   Action', Martin Robertson, 1973, p. 52.
10 Other work carried out by LARU indicates that CABs are viewed
   primarily as 'places where you go to be told who to go to for
   advice'. See for example P. Morris, J. Cooper and A. Byles:
   Public Attitudes to Problem Definition and Problem Solving,
   'Br. Jnl Social Work', 3, 3.
11 The SBAT clerks send an explanatory leaflet entitled 'Notes on
   Tribunals' to appellants when acknowledging their appeals.
   When this research was conducted the leaflet told appellants
   that 'Legal Advice is obtainable under the Legal Advice Scheme
   details of which can be obtained from Citizens Advice Bureaux
   or the Law Society's Legal Aid officer.' This leaflet was revised in January 1975 and the relevant passage now reads:
       Under the Legal Advice and Assistance Scheme a Solicitor
       can advise you on the preparation of your appeal and can
       draw up written submissions on your behalf. Details of
       this scheme can be obtained from the Citizens Advice Bureaux
       or the Law Society's Legal Aid offices.
   Our findings suggest that appellants have difficulty understanding official documents and language and that the vital
   importance of attendance is not made sufficiently clear.
13 These figures refer to appellants interviewed and the figures
   are much higher than was the case at observed hearings (15 per

cent, 18 per cent and 19 per cent respectively).   It will be
remembered that the sample of interviewed appellants was
structured to give a relatively high proportion of representa-
ted cases.   To this extent the views expressed may not apply
generally.

14   For a description of the work undertaken by the Free Representation Unit and its high success rate, see 'LAG Bulletin',
November 1973, p. 240.

15   S. Rees, and F. Edwards, in their article Power and Influence
in Social Work, 'Social Work Today', Vol. 3, no. 21, 25
January 1973, p. 19, call for social workers to have 'legal
training in knowledge of citizens' rights and the means of
ensuring that such rights are met'.

16   Bell, op. cit., p. 40:   'We would rate trade union officials as
the most effective representatives.'

17   See Appendix B, table B.3.

CHAPTER 7   SOME CONCLUDING COMMENTS

1   See pp. 9-11 for a more extended discussion of these issues.
2   For a discussion of the methodology, see pp. 14-28.
3   For a discussion of these issues, see the contributions of
P. Morris, R. White and P. Lewis in 'Social Needs and Legal
Action', Martin Robertson, 1973.
4   Note how many of the recommendations of the Franks Committee
have either not been implemented, or only partially so.   See
pp. 32-9.
5   See pp. 40-1.
6   See pp. 42-4.
7   'Rent Act 1974'.
8   For a review of the relevant literature, see J. Jowell, 'The
Legal Control of Administrative Discretion, 'Public Law',
Autumn 1973.
9   Ibid.
10   See pp. 44-6.
11   It is disconcerting to find that more than six months after the
Lord Chancellor's suggestion was made, no further plans have
emerged to put this extension of Legal Aid into operation (July
1975).
12   See chapter 6, pp. 56-70.
13   It is perhaps significant that the Lord Chancellor's Committee
on Legal Aid and Advice, Report 1973/4, is antagonistic to the
notion of 'class actions' and even in relation to law centres
states that:
   responsibility to a local community can easily come to mean
   a partisanship on behalf of a sectional interest within the
   community, stirring up political and quasi-political con-
   frontation far removed from ensuring equal access to the
   protection of the Law. (pp. 39-40)

BIBLIOGRAPHY

BOOKS AND ARTICLES

ABEL-SMITH, B. and STEVENS, R., 'Lawyers and the Courts', Heinemann, 1967.
ABEL-SMITH, B. and TOWNSEND, P., 'The Poor and the Poorest', Fabian Society Pamphlet, 1965.
ANDERSON, R.R., 'Representation in the Context of the Juvenile Court', Routledge & Kegan Paul, 1977.
BANKS, O. 'The Sociology of Education', Batsford, 1968.
BELL, K., 'Tribunals in the Social Services', Routledge & Kegan Paul, 1969.
BELL, K., Advice, Assistance and Representation Before Tribunals, University of Birmingham Conference Paper, April 1974.
BELL, K., 'Research Study on Supplementary Benefit Appeal Tribunals, Review of Main Findings: Conclusions: Recommendations', HMSO, 1975.
BELL, et. al., National Insurance Local Tribunals: A Research Study. 'Journal of Social Policty', vol. 3, part 4, 19XX.
BEVERIDGE, W., 'Social Insurance and Allied Services', HMSO Cmnd 6406, 1942.
BRIDGES, E., SUFFRIN, B., WHETTON, J. and WHITE, R., 'Legal Services in Birmingham', University of Birmingham, Institute of Judicial Administration, 1975.
BULL, D., Living Beneath the Clothes Line, 'Guardian', 7 December 1973.
BYLES, A. and MORRIS, P., 'Unmet Need: The Case of the Neighbourhood Law Centre', Routledge & Kegan Paul, 1977.
CAVENAGH, W.E. and NEWTON, D., 'Administrative Tribunals: How People Become Members', 'Public Administration', Summer 1971.
Conservative Party, 'Rough Justice', Conservative Political Centre, 1968.
CULP DAVIS, K., 'Discretionary Justice', University of Illinois Press, 1971.
DONNISON, D.V. (ed.), 'Essays on Housing', Codicote Press, 1964.
FLOUD, J.E., HALSEY, A.H. and MARTIN, F.M. , (eds), 'Social Class and Educational Opportunity', Heinemann, 1956.
FULBROOK, J., 'The Appellant and His Case', Poverty Research Series, CPAG, 1975.

FULBROOK, J., BROOKE, R. and ARCHER, P., 'Tribunals: A Social Court?', Fabian Tract 427, December 1973.
GOMM, R., The Claimant as Mendicant, 'Social Work Today', vol. 5, no. 12, 19 September 1974.
GRACE, C. and WILKINSON, P., 'Negotiating the Law: Legal Phenomena in Welfare Provision', Routledge & Kegan Paul, forthcoming.LIS
HARRISON, P., The Tribunals of the Welfare State, 'New Society', 22 November 1973.
HERMAN, M., 'Adminstrative Justice and Supplementary Benefits', Occasional Papers on Social Administration, no. 47, Bell, 1972.
HODGE, H., Techniques for Tribunals - 1, 'Legal Action Group Bulletin', December 1973.
HOOD, R., 'Sentencing in Magistrates' Courts', Stevens, 1969.
JOWELL, J., The Legal Control of Administrative Discretion, 'Public Law', Autumn 1973.
LAW SOCIETY, 'Second Memorandum on Legal Advice and Assistance', Council of the Law Society, 1969.
LISTER, R., 'Justice for the Claimant', Child Poverty Action Group, 1974.
LISTER, R., 'Review of Tribunals; A Social Court?' 'Poverty', no. 29, Summer 1974.
LYNES, T., 'Welfare Rights', Fabian Tract 395, 1969.
MARRIS, P. and REIN, M., 'Dilemmas of Social Reform', Routledge & Kegan Paul, 1967.
MARSHALL, T.H., 'Social Policy', Hutchinson, 1965, revised 1970.
MORRIS, P., WHITE, R. and LEWIS, P., 'Social Needs and Legal Action', Martin Robertson, 1973.
MORRIS, P., COOPER, J. and BYLES, A., Public Attitudes to Problem Definition and Problem Solving, 'British Journal of Social Work, 3, 3.
MOSER, C.A. and KALTON, G., 'Survey Methods in Social Investigation', Heinemann, 1971.
PEARSON, P. 'A New Deal for Furnished Tenants', Shelter, 1973.
REES, S. and EDWARDS, F., Power and Influence in Social Work, 'Social Work Today', vol. 3, no. 21, 25 January 1973.
ROETHLISBERGER, F.J. and DICKSON, W.J. 'Management and the Worker', Harvard University Press, 1939.
SINFIELD, A., 'Which Way to Social Work?', Fabian Society Pamphlet, 1969.
'Social Work Today', vol. 4, no. 6, 14 June 1973.
SOCIETY OF LABOUR LAWYERS, 'Justice for All', Fabian Research Series 273, 1968.
STREET, H., 'Justice in the Welfare State', Stevens, 1968.
TITMUSS, R., Welfare 'Rights', Law and Discretion, 'Political Quarterly', April 1971.
WRAITH, R.E. and HUTCHESSON, P.G., 'Administrative Tribunals', Allen & Unwin, 1973.

GOVERNMENT PUBLICATIONS

'Report of the Interdepartmental Committee on Rent Control', HMSO, Cmnd 6621, 1945.
'Report of the Donoughmore Committee', HMSO, Cmnd 4060, April 1932 (reprinted 1966).

'Report of the Committee on Administrative Tribunals and Enquiries',
HMSO, Cmnd 218, July 1957.
'Report of the Committee on Housing in Greater London' (Milner
Holland), HMSO, Cmnd 2605, 1965.
'Rent Act 1968', HMSO, May 1968.
'Department of Health and Social Security Annual Report 1973',
HMSO, Cmnd 5706, July 1974.
'Social Trends', no. 4, Central Statistical Office, HMSO, 1973.

OTHER PUBLICATIONS

'Annual Report of the Council on Tribunals', 1971/2 and 1972/3.
'Legal Aid and Advice, Report of the Law Society and Comments and
Recommendations of the Lord Chancellor's Advisory Committee',
1972/3 (twenty-third report), HMSO, 1973.
'Legal Aid and Advice, Report of the Law Society and Comments and
Recommendations of the Lord Chancellor's Advisory Committee',
1973/4 (twenty-fourth report), HMSO, 1974.